FLING WIDE THE DOORS OF THE UNCONSCIOUS

...trying to interpret a dream (that is, trying to abstract a message from it), although a natural and useful exercise, is but an imperfect approximation of recapturing the total understanding that must have accompanied the original dream experience. The dream story itself is the most perfect revelation of the truth of the dream. We can try to "see" with the eyes of the dream story, using a variety of techniques such as the ones I will present in this book.

Henry Reed

D1002705

There are many pathways to the New Age
Ballantine Books
for the body, mind, and spirit

GETTING HELP FROM YOUR DREAMS

Written and Illustrated by

Henry Reed

BALLANTINE BOOKS • NEW YORK

ACKNOWLEDGMENTS

Portions of this book have appeared previously, in different form, in the following sources whose copyright holders are gratefully acknowledged:

"The Art of Remembering Dreams." *Quadrant*. Summer, 1976. Copyright © 1976 C. G. Jung Foundation for Analytical Psychology.

"Dream Incubation: A Reconstruction of a Ritual in Contemporary Form." *Journal of Humanistic Psychology*. Fall, 1976. Copyright © 1976 The Association for Humanistic Psychology.

"Sundance: Inspirational Dreaming in Community." In Joseph Long (Ed.). *Extrasensory Ecology: Parapsychology and Anthropology*. Copyright © 1977 The Scarecrow Press.

"The Art of Dream Realization." *Dream Network Bulletin*. February, 1983. Copyright © 1983 by Chris Hudson.

"Getting Help from Dreams." *Venture Inward*. September, 1984. Copyright © 1984 Association for Research and Enlightenment, Inc.

ISBN 0-345-35511-3

This edition published by arrangement with Inner Vision Publishing Company

Manufactured in the United States of America

First Ballantine Books Edition: October 1988

CONTENTS

CHAPTER ONE

My Personal Story

Can we get any help from our dreams? Are dreams really any more than a rehash of the day's experiences? Could it actually be true that dreams can inspire us, provide guidance, even healing? If so, how can we ever know how to correctly interpret them? Science claims that dreaming is somehow necessary to our biological survival. Yet if remembering those dreams, not to mention correctly interpreting them, were the critical component of dreaming's survival value, then our species would long ago be extinct. Few of our dreams are remembered, and fewer still are understood. The critical value of dreams must lie elsewhere.

I believe that the essence of the dream is the *story* we experience during the night—*the experience of the dream changes us*. The guidance dreams provide, the help they give, is produced by the effect of the dream experience, remembered or not, upon our being. That's what I've come to understand from my own experience.

I was first introduced to the value of dreams by a

good friend of mine, an artist whom I held in special esteem, who shared with me how his dreams were enriching his life. He told me, for example, how he had first seen his inexpensive, but beautiful, oceanside studio in a dream, and then located it in town after some searching.

It was 1968 and I was preparing for my Ph.D. research examinations at U.C.L.A. Reading about dream psychology at that time, I learned that our oft-forgotten dreams were regarded as a natural, necessary and regular part of the sleep cycle, but the specific value of dreams remained undetermined. A few psychologists claimed they could deduce insights into a person's deep personality structure from dreams, as if dreams were meaningful symptoms. One psychiatrist, Carl Jung, claimed to have found something more than mere symptomatic meaning in dreams. He wrote that dreams have symbolic value, that more than simply reflecting the personality, dreams point beyond the individual to a system of guidance within life itself. But Jung, too, gave the impression that interpreting dreams was a magician's art.

While I had been studying dreams as a clinical phenomenon of ambiguous reputation, my artist friend was actively engaging his dreams as an extension of his creativity. He introduced me to the work of Edgar Cayce, who suggested that if you or I were to make an active attempt to become involved with our dreams, we would become the best interpreter of our own dreams and would be led to know how to receive the dream's help. What a different perspective! My friend's stories of his dreams were exciting and gave me a sense of great new possibilities. Being able to use dreams as an instrument of guidance, as if having an internal compass to point the way, had an irresistible appeal for me.

It was on such a note of inspiration that I finally dedicated myself to seek my dreams. I wanted to overcome my amnesia for them. As a New Year's resolution I began: I bound together a sheaf of papers into a handmade journal and covered it with some attractive material. I wrote a dedication prayer in the journal, asking that through dreams I might be able to see through the fog of my life. I wanted to connect with any meaningful life plan that might be within me. New Year's Day, 1969, was to be the first day of my new life!

I awakened that next morning without recalling any dreams. I tried the day after, but with no luck. I kept my journal by my bedside every night, night after night, but still with no success. It was disheartening but I persisted. Beyond my abstract, intellectual curiosity about dreams, I had good reason to persist. I had personal need. I was a troubled person, searching for something that would allow me to feel good about myself, something to give me a sense of direction and a new lease on life. I was 25 years old at the time, in the seventh year of my career as an alcoholic. I didn't know it at the time, but the effects of the alcohol were making it very difficult for me to remember my dreams.

It wasn't until sometime in March, over three months later, that I finally did remember a dream. I almost didn't remember it! I was already out of bed, groping in my closet for a shirt, when I remembered something about a flying goat. Aware that it wasn't an ordinary memory, but perhaps something of a dream, I sat back down on the bed and it gradually came back to me. I wonder how different my life might be today had I not been given a second chance to remember that dream. Here it is:

"I am camping in a tent on the land of an Old Wise Man. This land is his special sanctuary and I feel very grateful to be here. I am standing in the barnyard face to face with the Old Man. His deep eyes fix my gaze and I feel his presence quite strongly. I then notice behind him a flying goat! Yes, indeed, this place is special, and magical. The goat flies back and forth, a few feet off the ground, around the barnyard, then flies off into the barn, not to be seen again. Then to my left I see a haystack, and lying there an empty bottle of wine. I realize that someone has been there sneaking a drink. I say to the Old Man, 'Hey, look at that!—there's a drunk on this property, sneaking around to drink. We've got to find him and get rid of him, kick him out! He doesn't belong in such a special place as this.' But the Old Man faces me patiently, his deep eyes penetrating my innermost self, and replies, 'Henry, that man is a guest of mine, and was invited here long before you arrived. I put that wine there myself, to lure him in so that I can feed him.' I look back at the haystack and see an empty jar of mayonnaise and an empty bag of potato chips. Potato chips and mayonnaise, I wonder—what kind of food is that? I guess my image of a wise man would have him serving health food. But my presuppositions are brushed aside, for in the presence of the Old Man's generous acceptance of the drunkard, as mysterious as it may seem to me, my own self-righteousness sticks out in embarrassing and shameful contrast. I feel exposed and can't look the Old Man in the eye anymore. I wander off back into the forest and return to my little round tent."

This first dream proved very important and from the moment it was first recalled, it played upon my waking mind. Was the goat a symbol of my astrological sign, Capricorn? I wondered. There was a drunk in the dream—could that relate to my own drinking? As I asked myself questions I couldn't answer, I was discovering just what it is like to puzzle over the meaning of the images in a dream. I couldn't make much sense of my dream, but one thing stood out: the face of that Old Man and my feelings while talking with him. His intentions for the drunkard seemed very puzzling to me, but clearly my own attitude was inappropriate—my feeling of shame over being so righteous and uppity was a vivid memory from the dream. The idea that the Old Man purposely left wine for the drunkard as bait suggested to me that perhaps there was some *purpose* or *meaning* to my problem drinking that I just couldn't see. Yet the food being left for the drunkard—potato chips and mayonnaise—seemed so peculiar that I had a hard time accepting that it might make any sense. The question of meaning was left unresolved. But I no longer felt quite comfortable being so judgmental about my drinking.

This reaction was my first clue about getting help from dreams. A meaningful interpretation of the dream was not available. Instead, it was the natural, emotional effect of the dream upon me that proved important.

The impact of the dream upon me was that I tried to be accepting of my drinking and continue my quest for dreams. The former was much easier than the latter. I still found dreams hard to recall. I wasn't able to record another dream until July, and after a whole year, I was only on page three of my dream journal. I graduated from U.C.L.A., accepted a faculty position at Princeton University, and continued to recall only an occasional dream. That next summer I took a vacation and devoted myself exclusively to remembering my dreams. I would sleep late and then spend at least an hour when I awakened recalling as much of my dreams as possible. It took me that much work to catch on to how to recall them.

I gradually improved my dream recall to the point that it would take me several hours each day to write out my dreams fully from my morning notes. From my work that summer, I discovered some interesting subtleties about memory for dreams (they are summarized in Chapter Two, "The Art of Remembering Dreams"). During that time I began to develop an idea that we can get some help from dreams simply by remembering them. I reasoned that if the dream experience was meant to affect us, then by remembering the dream experience over and over again during the day, the impact of the dream would be strengthened.

That fall I decided to do a more formal study. In an experimental course, students and I developed a way to measure the results of our efforts trying to remember our dreams. Using this measuring scale we were able to prove that remembering dreams was a skill that could be learned. In a published report of our work, "Learning to Remember Dreams," I also noted our other finding, that after having learned how to recall dreams, we don't necessarily remember any unless we make the effort to do so.

While I continued to record my dreams, my drinking began to create problems for me I couldn't ignore. I suppose my story as an alcoholic is typical: repeated confrontations with the problems brought on by my drinking were met with repeated vows to quit drinking. These vows would then be quickly forgotten as my compulsion got the better of me, until finally that moment came of "bottoming out." I sunk into the despair of the truth: I knew that I would never voluntarily quit drinking—I loved it too much! I felt totally helpless and sullenly contemplated my future as an unredeemable, drunken bum.

One night, feeling very lonely and sorry for myself, I drank myself to sleep, only to find myself awake a few hours later, lost in uncontrollable sobbing. My crying was the carryover of this dream:

"I am amidst a crowd of people. We are looking up into the sky. It is night and yet the sun is up and acting strangely. Rays of light shoot out in all directions across the sky. An eerie tension unites the crowd and the sky. Out from the sun flies a glowing object. As it descends from the sky it appears to be a dove. The dove flies overhead, then zooms right down to me and nestles in my chest. I cry aloud, releasing tears of joy and relief. 'Somebody loves me!'"

The crying was still with me when I awakened from the dream. Afterwards I felt calmer inside, and felt as if there might still be hope. Again, it was the emotional impact of the dream, not any interpretation, that proved helpful.

Feeling I might be worth saving, I decided to seek psychotherapy. I remembered a Jungian therapist who I had heard lecture once before. When I had questioned her about my dream of potato chips and mayonnaise, her intriguing reply was, "The wine is the spirit." When I called for an appointment, I learned that her schedule was full, and it would be over a month before we could meet. In the meantime, I began to attend some meetings of Alcoholics Anonymous.

I was in for a surprise at these A.A. gatherings. Around my friends and peers, who were confounded by my drinking, I felt the loneliness of a stranger in a strange land, and I made no sense to myself. At the A.A. meetings, however, people spoke in a language that I immediately recognized and understood, and I felt myself reflected in their stories. By my third meeting, I accepted the fact that I was an alcoholic. Even though I didn't know how I would ever stop drinking, I was nevertheless strangely relieved. I realized that all the guilt trips and other torments I had suffered were not an expression of my individual personality, but instead were an expression of the personality of alcoholism. I likened it to a person unknowingly caught in a whirlpool, who feels scared and guilty for always spinning around in circles. But when the source of the predicament is realized, the feelings of foolishness and guilt are relieved, because it's not your fault when you're caught in a whirlpool, you're going to spin around helplessly until you are released.

One day soon thereafter, on my way home, I stopped by the liquor store to pick up my evening ration. But when I grabbed for a bottle, something inside me hesitated. I couldn't do it. I didn't understand what was happening, but finally I left the store empty-handed, thinking I would return later. But I didn't return. That evening, a mood of sadness descended on me, because I realized I couldn't drink anymore. I was surprised and somewhat put out. I hadn't yet decided to quit drinking—what was going on? I tried to make sense to myself about how I was feeling. I remember explaining to someone that I felt as if I were standing on the edge of a cliff, wanting very much to jump off, but realizing that there were plants back home that needed watering—who would water them if I jumped? Longing to jump into that bliss of release, but reluctantly accepting the responsibility of being needed at home, I sadly returned. My drinking career had ended.

But how? By whom? I hadn't decided to quit. I never would have done that! I didn't want to quit, ever. So what had happened? I didn't know. All I knew was that drinking was no longer an option for me and I felt sad about it. By then I had begun psychotherapy, and when I told the therapist what had happened, she did not seem at all surprised. She encouraged me to continue going to A.A. meetings. She surmised that I had been able to let go of drinking because I knew, at an unconscious level, that what I was seeking in booze would be found through our work in psychoanalysis. Maybe she was right. Only years later would I better understand what she meant. But at the time, at the beginning of therapy, at the beginning of my strange new career as a non-drinking alcoholic, I was a mystery to myself.

Much later I was to discover a garbled entry I had made in my dream journal just before my drinking disappeared. In this dream, I am at my grandmother's house, and I find a bottle of whiskey in the kitchen cupboard. I push it away, saying to myself that such stuff shouldn't be left in the reach of little children. Perhaps this dream, which I only vaguely recalled, represented an inner decision. In any event, it is the closest I have ever come to finding any act of "will," anything resembling a "decision" to quit drinking. Actually, I experienced my quitting not as something I did myself and could be proud of, but as something that happened to me, something I found out about after the fact.

Meanwhile, my research on dreams continued. I had learned from that first experimental class that it was hard for the students to maintain their interest in dreams without being able to interpret them or otherwise find some meaningful way to interact with them. Interpreting dreams was still very difficult for me so I searched for some alternatives. I had become more interested in Jungian theory, and had come upon a book by a Swiss psychiatrist, Carl Meier, *Ancient Incubation and Modern Psychotherapy*, about the cult surrounding the Greek god, Asklepios, who performed healings during the dream state. Sleep sanctuaries were created in his name, such as at Epidaurus. People with illnesses would sleep in these temples and have dreams that healed their afflictions. These dreams did not need interpretation, for the dream experience itself was the curative factor. Dream incubation appealed to me as it confirmed my own feeling that the dream must be sufficient itself to accomplish its purpose. I made arrangements to spend my sabbatical leave from Princeton at Dr. Meier's laboratory, the C.G. Jung Sleep and Dream Laboratory, in Zurich, Switzerland. There we explored many different types of experimental designs for studying problem solving in dreams. Returning to Princeton, I supervised student projects in my laboratory trying to implement some of these ideas. Inwardly, however, I felt dissatisfied with this research. Then I received an invitation to conduct dream experiments at the youth camp run by the Association for Research and Enlightenment, Inc., the nonprofit organization developed around the work of Edgar Cayce. Contemplating an outdoor setting for dream research among people predisposed to value their dreams inspired me and gave me the necessary impetus to design an experimental ritual of dream incubation.

On my way to camp I developed a plan to gather the campers together and tell them stories of the wonders of Asklepios, and speculate about the possibility of dream healing today. Since in the ancient days, a person could not sleep in one of the sanctuaries without a prior dream of invitation from Asklepios, I would tell the campers to watch their dreams for signs they were to undergo dream incubation. Only those who had such a dream should consider going any farther. For a sanctuary I bought a tent, an aesthetically pleasing, dome-shaped tent that would become the "dream tent." The design for the incubation procedure, briefly, was to engage the participant, the incubant, in a series of activities that would place the person in roughly the same frame of mind that must have existed in the ancient Greek pilgrim who was seeking a healing in one of the sanctuaries of Asklepios. The incubant was to imagine someone for whom he had tremendous respect as a healer or wise person, and to imagine the tent as a sanctuary located somewhere the person thought would be full of healing vibrations. I would then engage the person in a day of role-playing activities, in which the person would dialogue with his healing figure concerning the problem for which he sought help. That night, the person would sleep in the tent to have a helpful dream. That was the plan.

13

I arrived at camp, erected the tent, but when the time came to approach the campers with my plan, I got cold feet. I felt guilty and inadequate. Who was I to propose such an experiment? Things such as incubations were essentially initiation mysteries, processes that were handed down from master to initiate. I had not been initiated by anyone. It felt like I had made all this stuff up. I decided that the best thing to do was either to take down the tent, or if I left it up, to indicate simply that it was a fun place to sleep if you wanted to get away from the crowd and focus on your dreams.

I felt disappointed and depressed over my decision. But then, out of the blue, I remembered a disgusting joke I used to tell when I was a kid. It went like this:

There was a man with a terrible illness. He had scabs all over his body and these scabs were filled with pus. Every few days the man would peel off his scabs and put them into a bag. Then he would drain off the pus into a jar. Then he would store both of these in his closet. One day, a friend came to visit, wandered into that closet, and got himself locked in. It was three days before the man happened to open up the closet door. When he did so, his friend came stumbling out of the closet, saying, "Thank God! I would have starved if not for those blessed potato chips and mayonnaise!"

Yuk! Potato chips and mayonnaise! So *that* was the meaning of that perplexing image in my first dream! I was dumbfounded to have this long-buried memory suddenly pop into my mind at such a critical time. It had been over three years since I had had that dream, never understanding the reference to the strange food the Old Man was providing the drunk. Now, for some strange reason, I had recalled this childhood joke which obviously was the source of that dream image. I could then recognize, from my studies of symbolism, the significance of the image: it was a reference to the mystery of the homeopathic principle as declared by the Oracle of Apollo, "the wounder heals." It is the notion that an illness itself brings its own cure, that there is something in an illness that heals, if you will but incorporate it into your life. In my dreams, the Old Man used booze as a lure to teach me the secret of the healing power of woundedness.

I could see, from what booze had taught me, how this trick had worked. The spirits of alcohol came to rescue me from a one-sided existence. I realized that my life had been dominated by the intellectual pursuit of power as a means to deny my basic dependency upon factors in life beyond my personal control. When I reflected upon my "reasons" for drinking, I recalled that I always felt that life was too "concrete," and that I was always "scraping my knee" against its hard realities. Just as I had rejected the necessity of suffering, and had avoided it, so had I rejected the value of the Old Man's "food." I bit the bait on drinking, however, and found it, at first, to be a protective lubricant. But in time, the drink brought me face to face with my wounded knees, made me acknowledge the inescapability of my dependency, and made me give proper recognition to the importance of its spiritual basis. Finally, I had to accept the food, too. Rather than continuing to attempt to conquer life through power, like the willful captain of a motorboat, I had, after quitting drinking, gradually come to feel more comfortable as a skipper of a sailboat, utterly dependent upon the spirit of the winds and the moods of mother nature. The acceptance of that dependency upon spirit brought with it, paradoxically, a newfound sense of in-dependence and freedom as well as a feeling of being at home in the world. I had come to be grateful for my alcoholism as an affliction of the "gods" that only they could relieve, and thus it had become an initiation into the way of the spirit and the power of surrender.

All these ruminations brought me full circle back to my plans to pursue research on dream incubation. I realized that the method for dream incubation that I had so laboriously constructed was prefigured in my own first dream. The sacred place of the sanctuary, the revered benefactor of the Old Man, even the *tent* that I was now using—all these components had appeared in my dream! I remembered too that the god of dream incubation, Asklepios, was regarded as the archetypal "wounded healer," because his power of healing origi-nated from a wound. I had been profoundly mistaken to have assumed that it was my cleverness to have de-signed this experimental ritual, for I saw that I was unwittingly *acting out a dream*! What an irony, a hum-bling one at that, because while I had been stumbling around trying to figure out how to use dreams for cre-ative problem solving, all along my dream had been solving my problem without my knowing it! My dream provided me with a new life pattern based on an an-cient source of wisdom!

These surprising discoveries cleared away my inhibi-tions, and I went ahead with my plan. I announced the availability of the tent and began a program of re-search that was quite successful in demonstrating the continued operation of the miracle of dream incuba-tion. I'll give more detail about dream incubation later.

Looking back, I see that the synchronistic timing of

my recall of the old childhood joke, giving meaning to that critical image in the dream, coincided with the moment that the dream, and my original petition that led to the dream, were about to be fulfilled. I will always remember that critical moment of recollection in the dream tent. It was my first experience of what I later termed "Dream Realization." In Chapter 7 you'll read more about this approach to understanding a dream and get some hands-on training in how to use a dream journal to cultivate such moments of being able to see clearly through the eyes of a dream.

Needless to say, my own moment of dream realization inside the dream tent has shaped my personal view of dreams and how they help us. The inclusion of that image from a childhood joke into my dream, and the way it was apparently designed to work on me over the subsequent years, suggests to me an intelligence at work in the creation of dreams that designs the stories in such an exquisitely personally tailored fashion to arouse just exactly the desired effect, and proves to me that a dream is a meaningful experience that only the dreamer can fully appreciate. Thus, I am firmly in support of those who say, like Edgar Cayce and Carl Jung, that the dreamer is the best interpreter of the dream.

On the other hand, I believe now that trying to interpret a dream (that is, trying to abstract a message from it), although a natural and useful exercise, is but an imperfect approximation of recapturing the total understanding that must have accompanied the original dream experience. The dream story itself is the most perfect revelation of the truth of the dream. We can try to "see" with the eyes of the dream story, using a variety of techniques such as the ones I will present in this book. Also, we can simply allow the influence of the dream story to have its effect on us until we have changed sufficiently as a result of the dream that we find one moment that the meaning of the dream has been realized in life and that the dream no longer seems to require interpretation. In either case, I suggest that dream interpretation is essentially the art of fully remembering the dream.

Getting help from dreams, therefore, can be as simple, and as profoundly mysterious, as falling asleep to awaken a changed person. Even if we don't realize it for some time, it happens naturally every night.

CHAPTER TWO

The Art of
Remembering Dreams

It was with the problem of trying to remember dreams that I was first introduced to their mysterious ways. The extreme difficulty I had with dream recall created within me a certain reverent attitude toward dreams generally. It was with the belief that, somehow, the act itself of remembering the dream was an important bridge of communication between two realities that my approach to getting help from dreams developed. Remembering a long forgotten memory, bringing back to consciousness a secret, indwelling awareness of the meaning of "potato chips and mayonnaise" further strengthened in me my belief that the key to getting help from dreams was in how we remember them. In what follows, I will share with you the secrets I've learned about dream recall, and will explain an attitude toward remembering dreams that leads to a natural approach to receiving their help.

To describe the remembering of dreams as an art is

partially a confession of the mystery of the process. Yet, in many respects, learning to recall dreams is similar to learning any other skill. It requires motivation, an especially adapted vigilant strategy, an overcoming of possible resistance, and, above all, an attitude of confident patience. It is only when we practice these skills on a high level that the remembering of dreams becomes truly an art.

The Importance of Motivation

At first, natural curiosity about our dreams should supply enough motivation to make us try to remember them. We may wonder, for instance, what our dreams mean and what role they may play in our lives. By becoming aware of dreams and recognizing their importance we expand the domain of our conscious existence.

Still, once we turn our attention to dreams, they may disappoint us by appearing mundane or trivial and hardly worth the effort required to recall them. Moreover, if we compare ourselves with people who seem to have a natural ease in remembering dreams—dreams that are often more intriguing and imaginative than our own—we may find that curiosity is not enough to sustain our efforts to acquire a proficient memory for dreams.

When casual interest fails, we need a more compelling motive. Take, for example, the case of those people engaged in self-analysis or psychotherapy who have found their dreams to be a source of useful insights. They look to their dreams to find solutions to difficulties, to gain greater self-understanding, and to spark the hope for growth. These people have an intense interest in dreams and this sustains their attempt to remember them. Their example suggests that when dreams are seen as a means to some highly desired goal, there naturally develops sufficient motivation to recall them. The time and effort required to develop a fairly reliable memory for dreams is more willingly given when we hold our dreams in high regard and when we are firmly convinced that dreams are valuable and worth remembering.

The Potential Value of Dreams

Unfortunately, it is as difficult to prove scientifically that dreams can be meaningful or valuable as it is to prove that life itself has any meaning or value. Even though there is growing evidence that the biological aspect of dreaming has vital regulative functions in all mammalian life, dreaming must be approached, for our purposes, on a different level. An appreciation of life's potential worth and meaning can be gained by examining how people have lived their lives. Similarly, we may gain an appreciation of the potential value of dreams by considering how people have found them to contribute, for example, to their creative work.

Many creative persons in history have denied that their own efforts were alone responsible for their achievements. Attributing the fertile germ of their creation to involuntary processes, as if it were a gift from some source of intelligence other than their own, they pay respectful tribute to inspiration. Dreams, often the medium of such inspiration, have enlightened artists, philosophers and scientists.

Mozart, Schumann and Wagner all had dreams which provided some portion of their work. The same can be said of Dante, Voltaire, Tolstoy, Poe and Scott. We know from Goethe that *Faust*, and from Stevenson that *Dr. Jekyll and Mr. Hyde*, originated in dreams. But it is not only to literary works that dreams contribute. The essence of Descartes' philosophy came to him in a dream. Dreams were the well-spring of certain important discoveries in the sciences. In physiology it was the discovery of the chemical basis of nerve conductivity. In chemistry it was the formula for the benzene ring. In physics it was the common model for the atom. And Einstein, who himself kept notepaper by his bed to record his dreams, maintained that such intuitions as dreams provide were indispensable for fundamental insights into nature.

We may well ask, what is the source for the evident creative potential of dreams? Perhaps it is that dreams have access to long-forgotten memories and to perceptions which were originally only vaguely noted. Perhaps it is that dreams combine elements of experience in novel fashions, using bizarre imagery and/or powerful symbols. It is not only the especially gifted few, the creative geniuses, who find that they can sometimes be outdone by their dreams. We all have had dreams which seem to surpass our daytime talents. Our experience tells us, then, that dreams bear a creative potential for everyone.

Dreams Challenge Our Memory

Although the existence of dreams is a psychological reality, they typically defy direct observation. It should come as no surprise that because their realm is characteristically alien to our waking life, our memory for them is particularly fragile. The frequent elusiveness of dreams presents a formidable challenge to our memory.

Dreams seem to elude direct observation because when we are dreaming it is unusual for us to realize that we are doing so. When we do realize, we often respond to these unusual and particularly lucid dreams by an almost reverential appreciation. It is generally believed that by "awakening" to the dream, the dreamer is allowed to explore the mysteries of the dream realm and perhaps attain an enlightening experience of the paradoxical complementarity of reality and illusion. For most of us, however, the occasional realization that "this is only a dream" is quickly followed by waking up from sleep. Thus, since we usually find dreaming to be incompatible with consciousness of dreaming, we generally have access to our dreams only after they have left us. Consequently, our knowledge of dreams usually comes to us secondhand, from our recollection after awakening.

Awakening from a dream can itself be a rather puzzling experience, for the compelling reality of a vivid dream experience stands in bewildering contrast to the subsequent discovery that we have been actually lying in bed. The psychological reality of our dream experience can oppose the apparent reality of our daytime existence in such a way as to arouse our curiosity. There is a fable that expresses a metaphysical appreciation of this ambiguity.

Chuang Tzu dreamed that he was a butterfly. Since in his dream he did not know that he was anything else but a butterfly, he was happy and content to flutter from flower to flower. Later, he awoke to discover that he was not a butterfly but rather Chuang Tzu. But he was perplexed. "Am I really Chuang Tzu who dreamed he was a butterfly, or am I a butterfly who is now dreaming that he is Chuang Tzu?" The moral given is that there is a natural barrier between man and the butterfly: the transition between the two is what is meant by metempsychosis, that is, the transmigration of souls.

An adept in the art of Tibetan yoga is said to be able consciously to experience this transition. He attempts to maintain continuous consciousness while progressing from the state of wakefulness to falling asleep, then to dreaming and finally to re-awakening. Most of us, however, do not experience this underlying unity. We are accustomed to having our conscious existence interrupted by sleep. And when we awaken, we immediately reconnect quite naturally with our daily reality.

As we arise to confront the duties of the day, we can usually dismiss easily any lingering dream fragments as if they were meaningless fancies of a sleeping mind. Dreams invite such neglect for they usually appear discontinuous with each other and alien to our waking life. No wonder, then, that the dream is often rejected as incoherent nonsense and that it slips from our memory as we engage ourselves in the day's activities. Our memory system is not designed to retain nonsense. Being already overworked, it has little time to digest the strange forms of dreams, especially when they seem irrelevant to the needs and purposes of the day.

A more technical explanation of how dreams are forgotten is provided by experimental laboratory techniques which have been devised to observe the potential dreamer during sleep. Through the use of electronic instruments which monitor the bodily processes of the sleeper, it has been discovered that sleep passes through cyclical stages. About every ninety minutes the sleeper's brain-wave activity approaches that of wakefulness. The irregularity of the pulse and respiration suggests emotional arousal. Behind closed lids the eyes are moving rapidly as if observing some ongoing action. If the sleeper is awakened at this point, the person will usually report having been *dreaming*.

The discovery that dreaming occurs periodically through the night and that it is associated with a particular stage of sleep has significantly intensified the investigation of dreams. It is now generally acknowledged that if the sleeper is awakened immediately following the active stage of sleep, the person can usually recall a dream. However, this ability declines rapidly as the awakening is delayed. Consequently, in the morning the dreamer will have some difficulty in recalling the dreams he reported during the previous night. This indicates that we forget dreams not only after we awaken but also while we sleep.

People who complain that they never dream have been invited to sleep in dream laboratories. There the dreams are extracted during the night and in the morning the dreamers are presented with their recorded reports. It is clear, then, that when we awaken in the morning without a dream it is because we have forgotten.

Apparently the mind never sleeps, for when sleepers are awakened from other than the dream state, they will usually report that something was going on in their minds. Sometimes they will report that they were dreaming, but not so frequently as when they are awakened from the dream state of sleep. More often they will say that they were "thinking." This reported thinking activity resembles normal thought and typically relates directly to the sleeper's daytime concerns.

Why is it, then, that although we have been mentally active throughout the night, we experience our awakening as the emergence from unconscious sleep? Why should we be able occasionally to recall some of our dreaming but typically none of our thinking? This discrepancy is puzzling, since during the night we spend much more time thinking than we do dreaming. Moreover, the quality of our nocturnal thinking is perfectly compatible with that of our waking thought, whereas the quality of our dreaming is quite the contrary.

When we look for the factor that favors dreams and that affords them some tentative privilege to our memory, we find that it is the activation that is present during the dream stage of sleep. The dream state has been called activated or paradoxical sleep because of its resemblance to a waking state. It is, in some sense, a partial awakening. It is a psychological principle that a certain degree of arousal is necessary if we are to register something into memory. The arousal that occurs during the dream state—and it is absent during the other stages of sleep—is the probable basis for whatever ability we have to remember our dreams.

Vigilance for Dreams

If we wish to remember our dreams, we need more than a conviction of their value and an awareness of

28

the ease with which our dreams escape us. Vigilance is the basic strategy—a vigilance adapted to the peculiar elusiveness of dreams. In such a planned watchfulness, no time of day is unimportant, but let us turn first to the time when we actually dream.

Nocturnal vigilance means more than waiting until morning to try to recall our dreams. We have seen that laboratory investigations indicate that dreams are forgotten while we sleep. Thus, the morning recollection of dreams has inherent limitations. But the dream laboratory has something else to teach us. Experimental subjects have been trained with some success to wake themselves up after each dream. Such training depends both on hypnotic suggestion and also on the experimental conditioning methods in the laboratory. The results attained by these means provide an encouraging example of what it is possible to achieve in a short amount of time but with highly expert personal guidance. Relying on our own resources, we will be able to achieve as much, but for us it may take a bit longer.

Because we have seen that dreaming itself is a partial wakening, it comes as no surprise that we are capable of learning to wake up after a dream. As far as waking up several times during the night is concerned, we often do so, but we fall back to sleep so quickly that we have forgotten the dream by morning. Once we have seriously undertaken the challenge to remember our dreams, we are full of expectancy as we fall asleep at night. Our intention to be on the lookout for dreams and to remember them brings auto-suggestion into play. Our expectancy creates the basis for nocturnal vigilance. Our task, then, is to develop it and use it to our advantage.

Upon falling asleep we may experiment with a meditation from *The Tibetan Book of the Dead.* If we focus our desire for dreams into a concentrated "glow" in the back of the throat, we may then find that sleep will not erase our intention to notice our dreaming. The yogic phenomenology has an interesting psychophysiological parallel, for it is in the stem of the brain that the arousal during the dream state is controlled. Thus, by establishing mental contact with this center before falling asleep, its activation during dreaming may also awaken our intended vigilance.

But in any case, there may be a temporary difficulty. Occasionally we find that the intention to recall our dreams ruins our sleep. During the night we fidget and fuss. We may be anxious about our dreams, afraid that we may fail to remember them, but also perhaps afraid that we may succeed only to have terrible dreams. Given certain popular misconceptions about the nature of dreams, it is natural to experience some anxiety when we begin to try to remember them. More typically, however, it is simply the fact of our heightened expectancy which is to blame for a poor night's sleep. Any form of expectancy—some exciting or distressing event taking place the next day—can interfere with our sleep. But this should be no cause for concern, for we quickly become accustomed to the anticipation of our dreams.

The effects of vigilance during the night will probably first be evident to us in the morning when we awaken. We may recall having dreamed, but remember only that in the dream we reminded ourselves to "remember this dream." Here we have, in fact, taken advantage of the semiwakefulness accompanying the dream state to alert ourselves to remember the dream. At first it may appear that our vigilance is operating within the dream itself. What may have happened, however, is that we awakened to give ourselves this reminder, but since we awakened only so slightly and returned to sleep very quickly, our reminder subsequently appears to be a part of the dream experience itself.

The next stage in the development begins the night we discover ourselves lying in bed awake only to realize that moments ago we were dreaming. How can we take advantage of this awakening? Ideally, after each dream we would waken ourselves just enough to allow us to remember the dream in the morning, but without inhibiting our immediate return to sleep. This ideal state is best approached gradually, by experimentation, until we find the most efficient use of our vigilance; until, as it were, we can have our dreams and sleep, too.

Begin by using the nocturnal awakenings to rehearse the dream and so fix it in memory. A good method is to lie quietly with eyes closed and redream the dream in an attempt to memorize it. Then, having reviewed the dream with a confident reminder to recall it in the morning, it is easy to go back to sleep. This procedure can be perfected until we are able to recall dreams in the morning almost as completely as they were rehearsed during the night. But there are typical failings.

Sometimes we will experience an annoying feeling that the dream we recall in the morning does not compare either in clarity or completeness to the dream we remember having had during the night. In fact, there may remain only a disappointing fragment which refuses to yield to even our most patient efforts to expand it. And sometimes in the morning we will awaken to the frustrating discovery that we have a vague but

31

certain memory of having dreamed, but that the dream is beyond recall. Then we realize that while we were rehearsing the dream that night we drifted back to sleep. The nocturnal rehearsal method can fail us, then, either because of the difficulty with which the dream submits to memorization or because of an insufficient degree of wakefulness when we reviewed the dream. If this is the case, we can take another lesson from the laboratory approach and during the night make a written record of the dreams which awaken us.

For a few nights it might be a useful experiment to record in detail whatever dreams awaken us. But, in general, the degree of arousal and effort required to initiate and accomplish this task would leave us wide awake. So rather than abandoning our vigilance, we might do better to make brief notes that we can rely upon to deliver up our dreams in the morning. To do this successfully is probably the most efficient use of our vigilance. As we rehearse a dream that has awakened us, its most vivid aspects will suggest themselves as cues for recalling the entire dream. Notepaper, of course, should be kept conveniently close at hand. To arise, even slightly, from the relatively pleasant experience of rehearsing a dream to pick up a pen and paper to make notes will seem to require heroic moral effort. The physical effort needed to make notes must be minimized. Even a light is not necessary, for it is possible to write in the dark without much trouble. The slight fatigue from making these notes and the confident feeling of having secured the dream make it easy to drop back to sleep without further concern.

This approach is probably the most economical use of nocturnal vigilance. As we perfect the notation method, we will probably wake in the morning to discover two or three nocturnal records, but with only a dim recollection of having awakened during the night to make them. Quiet contemplation in the morning, supplemented by notes from the night, can, with practice, deliver on many mornings as many as five dreams.

Once we have embarked on a strategy of planned watchfulness, we must look carefully at the fragile transition between sleep and wakefulness in the morning. Even though we have made notes during the night, the moment of awakening in the morning is the most crucial opportunity to detect dreams. It is also true that at this moment our dreams may be lost. Dream images from the night seem very faint in the strong light of day. The awakening thought, "What do I have to do today?" is their most dangerous enemy. Our first task, then, is to condition ourselves so that when we awaken in the morning our first thought is for our dreams. Sometimes it may be helpful to verbalize our intention before falling asleep, but, in general, we can rely upon our desire to remember our dreams to be a sufficient reminder. Being so prepared, we will often find that our vigilance is rewarded by the discovery that we were dreaming just before we woke up. Often it is the last part of the dream that lingers in our mind. With careful attention to this fragment, the entire dream may be retrieved.

There is both a technique and an art to allowing a dream fragment to expand into an entire dream. It is of primary importance to avoid distractions which may interfere with detecting the dream. It is also important not to disturb the physical context in which the dream occurred. Therefore, one should remain motionless, in the same position as upon awakening, and keep the eyes closed. Get back in touch with the dream by re-experiencing the part that is recalled. Mull over the feelings evoked by the special mood of the dream as you examine each character and event. As we review a dream in this way, forgotten elements emerge. How this happens is unclear; it can be said only that one element of a dream must somehow remind us of another. But dreams cannot be hurried. We learn that we have to wait for remaining material to come of its own accord. So it is that how we wait becomes part of the art of remembering dreams.

When we try to recount the events of the previous day, our daily routine provides some structure to aid our efforts at reconstruction. But there seems to be no such routine in a dream. We may question the gaps in our memory of the dream but the only way we can fill these gaps is patiently to review the dream—and wait.

On some mornings we shall awaken without a clear feeling of a dream. Though we will probably be tempted to get up, we should, nevertheless, remain quietly in bed and wait. We might discover something to help us remember a dream. We may ask ourselves, "What does it feel like to wake up this morning?" If there is a mood, get in touch with it, savoring its special quality without trying to pin it down with words. Often a flickering fragment will appear which can then serve as a hook to retrieve the whole dream. Or perhaps there is an image or thought which catches our attention because of its unlikely character. This may be a clue to a dream.

But often there is nothing special until the moment comes when we suspect the presence of a hidden dream. It is as if we accidentally stumble upon the right combination in the static of the mind that places

34

us in momentary empathy with the feelings of the dream. Sometimes, too, there appears to be nothing at all, and then suddenly a dream unfolds before us. Such is the mystery of dreams. And that special quality of contemplation which crystalizes dreams dissolved in the hazy fog of the awakening mind also becomes part of the art.

After gleaning whatever dream images arise from our initial efforts, we should not yet give up the hunt. Memory for dreams is to some extent dependent on recreating the physical context in which the dream occurred. Try moving gently into each of the other positions in which you sleep and await additional dreams. It would seem as if the dream were stored in a code which is most intelligible when we are in the original posture of the dream. It has been found in the laboratory that when people roll over as they are awakened from a dream they have much more difficulty recalling the dream than when they are motionless upon awakening. Doubters can experiment for themselves by comparing their ability to re-experience a dream in different positions. Trying to recall a dream while in an inappropriate position can feel something like trying to write left-handed. It is useful, therefore, to explore our sleeping postures, for each may contain unique dream memories. Moreover, dreams of the same night are often linked in subtle ways, so that dream images gained in previous positions can be reviewed as lures for other dreams. Still waiting is of the essence.

It is, then, also worthwhile to turn to whatever notes we made during the night and try to get in touch with the dreams they represent. Generally, each of these clues provides an easy recollection of a small aspect of the dream and as each of these is reviewed, the remaining parts of the dream gradually appear. To be thorough, we should carry these dream images also through each of our sleeping positions, for they may attract further dream memories.

Developing the habit of patient, quiet contemplation in the morning is vitally important to our learning to recall dreams. Our experience will show that if we spend some time lying in bed waiting, a hasty assumption that we have remembered no dreams will prove to be incorrect. It is, in fact, during such quiet, meditative efforts that we gradually realize the creativity inherent in the process of retrieving dream memories.

Even after we rise in the morning we should continue to be on the lookout for dreams, for it is not unusual for a dream memory to flash into the mind later in the day. Although the reason for such a sudden appearance is not always clear, it seems that an object or an event similar in some way to an element of the dream, or which evokes a reaction in us similar to a reaction we had in the dream, stimulates our memory. More often, the dream itself does not appear, but instead we encounter a vague feeling of being reminded of something. It is as if a dream were delicately balanced on the edge of the mind, almost about to roll into view. We need utmost care to tease it into consciousness, for it is as if the slightest jerking movement might jar it back into oblivion. Here again we find a use for the art of retrieving such fleeting images, for the phenomenon is so subtle that it is likely that we overlook many interesting instances because of our lack of attention.

The Daytime Attitude Toward Dreams

Our desire to encourage spontaneous dream memories is just one of the reasons that during the day we should not forget or ignore our dreams. An often neglected aspect of developing a memory for dreams is the attitude that we have toward them during the day. The motivation that is necessary to our remembering dreams depends upon our respect for their potential values. If we do not properly value our dreams, our motivation for recalling them will slowly fade away. We must therefore conscientiously maintain an attentive, devoted, curious admiration for our dreams. This particularly fruitful attitude toward our dreams is difficult to express either in theory or action.

Perhaps we might say that it is as if our dreams were the appearance of an elusive, would-be lover. We cannot demand that she do our bidding or conform to our expectations. Even though she may frustrate or disappoint us, we dare not criticize her mysterious ways. So we allow her to come in any manner that she will and we are grateful when she visits us. What other way is there to win such a lover?

Another analogy may be helpful here. Suppose that dreams were utterances of an infant learning to speak. We are delighted at baby's first words. Even though we can only guess at what he might be saying, we do not scorn or ignore him—nor do we doubt his potential for future eloquence. Instead, we applaud his efforts, and, by our attention, encourage him to continue speaking. We even take special note of his words and are all too eager to tell our friends about his speech. Thus we should not ignore even the least dream fragment as seemingly insignificant, nor should we disregard our dreams as meaningless even though they may puzzle us. Rather, we should give each one careful attention and with each develop an appreciative familiarity. How else can we expect the child to say even greater things?

Not only do these two metaphors—the elusive lover and the speech of an infant—illustrate an attitude which will support our attempts to learn to remember dreams, they also suggest ways to actualize this attitude and warn us of some common resistances which we may encounter. The basic resistance, and it is one that may take many forms, is the tendency to reject our dreams. Although our reason for rejecting a dream is usually perfectly valid when considered on its own terms, through such rejections our dream recall is nevertheless inhibited. Therefore, we must periodically come to terms with the source of this resistance.

We may, for example, reject a dream outright. Upon awakening in the morning, we may say to ourselves, "Oh, that was nothing!" and carelessly toss aside a lingering dream image which otherwise might have provided a memory for a dream. When we are seriously trying to recall our dreams, such judgments are ill-advised. Later in the day a rejected dream fragment may seem to be quite interesting after all, but then we will be disappointed to discover that we can no longer recall the dream.

We may also disregard a dream on the basis that our memory of it is too incomplete or confused. We may fall prey to philosophical doubt concerning the basis for trusting memory itself and we will confuse ourselves with doubts as to whether we dreamed at all. The subjective certainty which typically accompanies the initial, spontaneous recollection of our dream will fade with time and as the dream is scrutinized. Thus, it is better to record the first memory of the dream and let it go at that. There will always be time for later editorial revision and the original evidence will have been preserved.

Another reason for rejecting a dream is that it seems to be disappointingly short and apparently trivial. We may conclude that the dream does not contain much of value. In another instance, a dream may repel us because of its seeming incoherence or absurdity, or perhaps even because its contents offend us. But we should set aside our judgments and remember the dream. Even though our reasons may be valid, our developing ability to recall dreams is jeopardized each time we devalue one of them. Each time we ignore a dream, we reinforce the auto-suggestion that our dreams are not worth remembering—in effect, an instruction to ourselves to forget our dreams.

Still another source of our resistance is fear, a fear of what we may discover in our dreams. As amateur psychoanalysts we often assume that dreams can reveal only our negative qualities and serve only to destroy the convenient illusions we have about ourselves. But we should not allow this preconception to prevent us from considering the positive possibilities as well.

A more typical source of resistance arises from the demands of our daily existence. Our dreams may seem to have little relevance to our immediate concerns and we may feel that the time it takes in the morning to pay proper respect to our dreams interferes with our desire to get a quick start on the day. Therefore, it is important for us to reaffirm the importance of dreams so that they can effectively compete for our attention.

Nevertheless, in spite of our best intentions, there will be periods when we do not remember our dreams. One may speculate as to possible causes for cycles in dream recall. Sometimes a dry spell is the result of a temporary condition, such as the pressures of an external situation, or the need to divert energy from self-preoccupation. But when we are reunited with our dreams, our previous experience in recalling them will make for a speedy recovery.

The Commemoration of Dreams

There are a number of ways to give attention to our dreams. First, maintaining a dream diary is essential. Having a special book for recording and preserving our dreams is a powerfully symbolic gesture of respect for them. A dream journal has the double advantage of sparing our memory the impossible task of storing all our dreams and at the same time providing us with a space in which to develop, by writing out, our realizations of the meanings in the dreams. As the book grows, it becomes more and more of a reference work. As someone once said, "The best book on dreams is the one you write yourself."

We may further wish to honor our dreams by giving them artistic expression. It is often a good idea when we record our dreams also to include illustrations and diagrams in the diary. Certain dreams or dream images may stimulate the production of a satisfying painting. But even doodles made in the dream journal while musing upon the dream may yield surprising results. It is also possible to create poetry and stories of fantasy from our dreams. Besides providing works of aesthetic value, creative writing from dreams can also promote a greater awareness of the significance of the dreams.

Another important way of giving attention to our dreams is simply to think about them during the day. As we ponder what we dreamed during the night, we will often find it stimulates further dream memories and sometimes new ideas emerge. Thinking about dreams is often a good way to test and develop our memory for them, for we will find it easier to recollect (without aid of our dream diary) the dreams we recalled that morning and on previous mornings, even dreams of the most loosely connected sort.

By keeping our dreams in mind, we invite our daytime experiences to remind us of our dream images. It's no accident when we are reminded of a dream. We gradually discover the natural associative context of our dreams and we find that our past dreams provide us with frequent metaphors for our ongoing experiences. These spontaneous, meaningful coincidences often lead us along a natural path of dream realization.

Another aspect of giving attention to dreams is the practice of occasionally talking over, or simply telling, our dreams with friends. Discussing our dreams helps us to overcome any shyness we may have about them and it also serves to give them an added importance. The opposite can also be true: a dream kept purposefully a secret develops a special value all its own. Yet if we dream of a friend, discussing that dream with the person gives us an opportunity to add a further dimension to our friendship. Although it might be true that we dream mostly of ourselves and that the friend in our dream represents some aspect of ourselves, discussing the dream with the other person may nevertheless yield some surprises.

The care we take to retrieve and reflect upon our dreams pays us rich rewards. Yet the creative potential in our dream life will develop in reality only to the extent that we take our dreams seriously enough to act upon them. As we gain appreciation for our dreams, they will cease merely to entertain us. They will begin to provide us with a source of hypotheses about ourselves and our environment. But only when we test these hypotheses by daily experimentation can we expect to exhibit the vitality that our dreams require in order to help us most. Like the difference between having an idea and making it work, living the understanding the dream brings is the crucial test in the art of remembering dreams.

The use of the term "art" might seem overdrawn unless we consider the nature of the creative process. Creativity is sometimes described as the ability to combine common elements into novel relationships. It is the ability to suspend for the moment our usual working assumptions so that new thought patterns can form that constitute the essence of creative functioning. Even though these new patterns appear vague and remote, entering into an empathic relationship with such potential sources of inspiration until they can clearly manifest is itself a creative act.

Creativity is also the process of bringing to light those invisible, autonomous promptings, the daimons of the dark, which normally hold us in their secret sway. Dreams are the daimons' playground, and our days are subsequently affected by their nocturnal activity. Remembering our dreams, then, becomes a creative process which offers us the opportunity to participate with increasing consciousness in the drama of life.

Each dream is a creative act. Dreams habitually disregard our everyday logic and typically surprise us with their juxtapositions. It is not only their tendency to dissolve rapidly, but also their alien quality that makes them elude retrieval. Remembering our dreams, commemorating them in our lives, then, is a creative art in which we can all become more or less proficient. It is worth the practice. At the very least, it offers us a way to develop our potential for creative functioning and it may offer us more than that. It has been said that a journey of a thousand miles begins with a single step.

CHAPTER THREE

Dreams Are a
Theater Experience

A dream is an experience we have while we are asleep. It becomes part of our personal history that shapes us and makes us who we are just as our experiences during the day become part of who we are. In particular, my perspective on dreams is that it is the *story* of the dream that changes us while we sleep. The dream story affects us in the same way that experiencing a play or a movie might change us. Reading stories, watching movies, seeing plays, having dreams—these all have personal value to the extent that they affect us, move us, change us. It is only natural to be affected by the stories we experience, whatever their form.

I would like to give you a feeling of permission to have a natural response to your dreams. In other words, if dreams are a natural experience, if their effect on us is as normal as the effect of experiencing a story, then it shouldn't require a lot of expertise to reap their benefit. Getting help from dreams can be as

She Dreams Me

natural as being moved by a theater experience.

Children love stories. They don't need an English teacher explaining the symbolism and pointing out the various complexities in order for them to appreciate a good story. Children will frequently ask to have their favorite story read to them again and again. Simply hearing the story is having an effect on the child. The child and the story are in direct, mysterious communication. The story is something the child wishes to experience over and over—even the bad and scary stories, such as the fairy tales that often are like gruesome nightmares. In their innocent and direct appreciation of stories, children have something to teach us about dreams. We should be able to gain as much from our dreams and in as simple and straightforward a manner as children grow from hearing stories. As stories, dreams have the drama of a theater experience.

The ancient Greeks were famous for their philosophy of drama and the way they incorporated drama into their lives. They considered it to be an important social process. They realized that bringing people together to see the plays had an effect on the society, releasing tensions that were difficult to deal with, uplifting people, training them in various ethical situations and issues. For the Greeks, drama and dreams were natural partners. At Epidarus, for example, both the theater and the dream incubation sanctuary were located within the same ceremonial center. They found that drama and the arts surrounding drama revealed the meaning of their humanity. Not too much has really changed in the last 2000 years—dreams, those nighttime dramas, still speak to those deep human issues that unite us.

What are some of the things in a play that move us?

What is it about the story? How do we see what the story is? How do we even understand story itself? We are never really taught to understand story, but it seems very natural to us. We naturally tend to perceive events in terms of meaning, and not just raw facts. Many psychological experiments have been created to demonstrate that in the act of perception, we bring "meaning" to the raw facts. One of my favorite examples of this was an animation demonstration by Fritz Heider. In the cartoon, there were only two dots in motion. The motion was programmed mathematically. As one dot moved, so did the other a short distance away. When people were shown the cartoon and asked what they saw, they invariably saw one dot "chasing" another. There was nothing in the raw facts of the cartoon that specifically designated the act of "chasing." The mind of the observer added the meaning to the raw facts. "Chasing" was a direct and immediate experience for the observer. People were shown a mathematical process, but they experienced a story—a chase scene. Experiencing events in terms of their meaning, in terms of a story, is very natural.

Besides being natural, experiencing events in terms of story can be very important to us. When *Roots* was dramatized on television, it was interesting that several times the hero would recite the story of his origins and how he had gotten to where he was. First there was Great Grandfather, who was a slave who came here, then there was the Grandfather, who did this and that, and so on. That was why he was here. Reciting that sequence was very important in giving him a sense of where he was and who he was. To the so-called primitive peoples, losing their heritage of the stories that tell how they came to be is as disastrous for them as it would be for us to lose our storehouse of scientific knowledge.

We each have our personal stories, the experiences we cherish, as well as the ones we wish we hadn't had, that make us who we are, that give us a sense of direction or meaning. It is these stories that we share with one another as we become friends. Generally, the abstractions and raw facts we share with one another—our astrological sign, our blood type, our scores on the Rorschach test, or our job title—reveal less about us than the stories we tell about ourselves. We naturally relate to one another in terms of common experiences, and we discover that commonality by exchanging stories with one another. Hearing a person's self-analysis may give us some understanding, but the stories the person tells give us a better feeling for the person. We can identify with the story and feel close to the person.

We are all familiar with the saying, "A picture is worth a thousand words." A picture tells a story; it arranges all the facts in a package that can be grasped instantly. In a similar fashion, a story is worth many explanations—a story tells it all! We can try to explain people, their behavior and their inner feelings by recourse to psychology, but a good story gets to the heart of the matter and is immediately understood. While we may scratch our heads for a while before an explanation sinks in (only to soon forget it), the meaning of a story is often immediately understood in an unforgettable manner.

Did you ever wonder why, if dreams are like messages, that they rarely occur in the form of explanations, lessons, lectures or letters? They are most often simply stories. We experience them like a play at the theater, or a movie. There is something very basic about the story in a play. Why did Shakespeare say the world was a stage and we were the characters on it? Life itself seems like a story. The story we call life is older than the invention of language, and so are dreams. It is more natural for dreams to appear as stories than as letters. Dreams are stories that we experience during the night and they have a direct and immediate effect upon us.

In dreams we can have the experience and be changed as a result of the experience. We can forget the experience but the change is there nevertheless. On that level the dream can go on accomplishing its goal without our attempting to understand it. I am not saying that interpretation is wrong. I am saying that there is a more basic level to a dream, it is very direct and we're all naturally very good at understanding it.

There is a statement, for example, that a dream that's not interpreted is like a letter that isn't opened. There is truth in that. Until a dream has been interpreted or accepted as personally meaningful, there remains a level of the dream that has not yet been acknowledged. But the dream has its own dimension of reality, too. Dreams are like a chiropractic adjustment. They *grab* us, they *affect* us, they *involve* us, and they *change* us. They shape us and we have been changed by them. And for that purpose interpretation is not necessary. The immediate reality of the dream is the story that is experienced.

For example, the night before doing something I had never done before, I was really scared and nervous, asking myself why I had ever agreed to take such a risk, but not knowing how to get out of it. That night I dreamed of my father. In the dream, he was going off to work. He had just taken a shower and put on a fresh suit. He smelled really good as he said goodbye to me and walked out the door. That dream was similar to a memory. I recall various times when dad would wear cologne and would smell so good. I would be proud of him as he went out on his job. The dream brought back those memories. It left me feeling good, thinking about it uplifted my mood. Although I didn't make the connection at the time, I realized later that the dream gave me the confidence to take the risk I had to take and perform the task I had agreed to.

The dream experience had its effect. The story of the dream, and the memories it evoked, did the job. True, the story can be interpreted. What does the story say? It is a story of confidence in meeting the outer world. In the story, my father does what dads do—he goes out into the world to support the family back home. There is dad, smelling like a rose. It is the father within us, that aspect that has knowledge and the confidence to use it, that can support those other aspects within us that need supporting, the more dependent sides of ourselves. In that sense my dream story contains archetypal, or universal, symbols. Yet I did not need to know any of that in order to reap the benefit of the dream. Dad's sweet smell of success was all the boost I needed.

There are so many theories about dreams today and so many books on dream symbols and how to interpret them. As science has become dominant in our culture, we tend to think like scientists, in terms of theories and explanations, even though scientific theory is devoid of human meaning, the kind of meaning that makes life worth living. And now we also have our science of dreaming. There seems to be so much to learn, so much psychological sophistication to develop, so much standing between us and our dreams. It gets very complicated, and we get self-conscious and nervous. Dreams seem to be too difficult to analyze, and we are afraid that we will miss the point of the dream or misinterpret it.

But can you imagine being afraid to go to a movie because of a fear that you couldn't figure it out? I cannot imagine someone saying, "Well, I don't want to go see *Ghostbusters* because I might not understand all the symbols." We're not afraid—we just go and enjoy the movie. If we can analyze the symbols, that's fine, and it will add to our appreciation of the movie. But it would be sad to avoid the experience of the movie for fear of not being able to analyze the symbols. Don't let a feeling of a need for sophistication make you miss out on your dreams. True, dreams may contain symbolism, analogy and metaphor; and there are, indeed, psychological dynamics and biological determinants in dreams. Nevertheless, dreams are given to us as stories. A dream is a theater experience that directly touches our sense of being.

When we respond to a dream directly, like a story, like a theater experience, what are the implications? What does it mean in terms of working with a dream, coming to enjoy it more or finding whether it has some application or practical value? How might we tap into that?

Instead of remembering a dream and immediately thinking of various symbols and what they might mean, first ask, "How do I feel after this experience?" "Do I feel excited or a little bit low?" "What is it that I desire?" "How does the story of the dream affect me?" Notice what we have to pay attention to in order to answer that question. Does it leave a certain mood or feeling? It may leave a certain appetite or desire or a lingering itch to accomplish or change something. What kind of an aftertaste is there to the dream?

For example, I had a dream in which I was standing on the running board on the side of a car. The car was going down the road really fast, and I was holding on for dear life. That was the dream. How did that leave me feeling? I was feeling scared in the dream; the motion was fast. It was nice to wake up and find myself in bed. I was stable; the bed was not moving; and that was a nice feeling. One of the effects of the dream was to somehow make me appreciate taking it easy or going slow or keeping my feet on the ground. The impact on me is that it slowed me down. It made me a little bit more security-conscious in some way.

After we have remembered a dream, it is important to remember it again and again and again, often calling it to mind during the day. If the dream is meant to be a story that affects us, that changes us, then by remembering it several times we can reinforce and keep that effect active. It is a way of reliving it. If some of the value of the dream is the experience of the dream, then we derive that value by remembering it over and over again. We will find, too, that by recalling dreams often, things will easily remind us of our dreams, because we have gotten used to bringing them to mind. And the thing that reminds us of the dream is telling us something about the meaning of the dream. There is a reason why that dream is brought to mind at this particular time, in this particular situation. It can be an easy and painless way to appreciate what some of our dreams mean, but we have to help that process out. If we remember a dream in the morning but then forget it, it is very difficult to be reminded of it later. However, if we ask, from time to time during the day, "What did I dream last night?" and then, if we relive it, that practice makes the process of recalling dreams at meaningful moments that much easier.

In trying to realize the value of simply remembering a dream and rehearsing it mentally, we often come up against the unpleasant dream. Who wants to remember an unpleasant or scary dream? Maybe it's okay for kids to want to hear a scary story over and over again, but we grown-ups have work to do and don't need the useless upset, right? Well, it is right that many dreams, in fact, are unpleasant. That, along with the fact that we don't seem to be able to survive without our dreams, suggests that the unpleasantness in dreams is serving a purpose. The purpose seems to be to help us realize or anticipate the negative consequences of some attitude or stance we are assuming in our life. The negative emotion in the dream is like a bad taste in our mouth in the morning. It automatically steers us away from the attitude we previously held or were contemplating. I don't know what freewheeling attitude I had the night before I dreamed of riding on the running board of the runaway car, but believe me, the next morning, I was a more humble person! The more I rehearsed that dream in my mind, the more humble my mood became. So even without knowing the intent of the dream, the specific aspect of my being that it was referring to, I assume the dream did its job and my rehearsing it helped it even more.

After remembering a dream, examining its emotional effect upon you as you rehearse it, the next important dimension to look at is the story itself, its theme or plot. What is going on in the dream? What is the essential plot? Let's examine the plot of a dream I had:

"I am standing in a barnyard, and I see that my horse has been tied to a tree. But the horse has gotten loose and is walking away. I want to holler after it, 'Wait!' But I can't think of the horse's name. I say, 'Charlie,' and then think, 'No, that's my dog.' I keep hollering different names, and I can't remember my horse's name. I think, 'Gee, it's just going to walk away and leave me.' I'm really feeling despondent; then I get a nudge and there's the horse. He's come back. I'm really happy and I put my arm around the horse and start singing to it. I sing some cornball songs that I'm making up in the dream. At one point I hit a real high-pitched note —la la—and both the horse and I roll over back-wards because he's singing, too. It's like 'horse laughter' because I'm being so corny. We're rolling on the ground together with our la la's."

That was the dream. What is the essential theme of that dream? Several possible ones are: Thinking something is getting away from me; finding something that I thought I had lost but that was there all the time; thinking I have to have control but finding control is unnecessary. (The statement about control might go a bit beyond what is actually in the dream. It is a good idea to keep to the story.) The theme is something that we are able to grasp all at once, in a single snapshot. So, I would say that the theme of my dream is that something I felt was lost was actually there all the time.

I had this dream the morning of a workshop on dreams and poetry. I was concerned because I had not given this workshop for a long time. In the past I had spent a lot more time writing poems from my dreams, playing around with them, making pictures and so on, but I hadn't been doing so much of that recently. I had this dream that morning and, in the course of giving the workshop, I used the dream to do my poetry work. It dawned on me that the dream was expressing that I had not lost something just because I hadn't been dealing with it for a long time; it was still there.

Working with a theme from a dream can be helpful, even if you find you can only abstract an approximate theme. Use the theme as a perspective by which to view your life situation. Ask yourself, "How does this theme reflect my current life situation?" What correspondence can you find between the theme of the dream and life events? If you were to use that dream theme to frame your perspective on your life, what would you find? What feelings or thoughts are evoked? For example, in my dream, the theme seems to reflect my feelings about my poetry ability. When I picture those feelings from the perspective of the dream theme, I experience some relief about the continued presence of my creative talents. Before I worked with the theme, the dream seemed unrelated to me. Once I abstracted the theme, I recognized immediately what aspect of my life was being portrayed.

Identifying the theme is not going to give us all there is to a dream, but it can give an awareness of what to orient to, the basic skeleton of the meaning. Then we can add little things on to it. An outline has value in that it gives some structure. We know what the basic structure is and what is simply detail. "Frustration" and "control" in my dream seem to be refining details for better understanding the basic notion that something seems to be getting away although it is there all the time. It is helpful to get used to thinking in terms of themes. The theme points to the critical or central truth that will give us some kind of orientation for working with the rest of the dream. Then we may want to go on to the details: frustration, the name of the horse, etc. Why was there a problem with names and not more about the horse not being tied up very tight? Why did I call it the names of my other animals? These things are little details we can work with better once we have a feel for the general structure.

Another aspect of a dream is its symbols, its characters. One thing that has always fascinated me about dreams is the symbolism. Often dream symbols are taken from the material of our waking life, as with my dream of "potato chips and mayonnaise." However, through the ages one of the reasons people have maintained such an interest in dreams is that images sometimes appear which we have never experienced in our waking life. Where do these images come from? One theory says we come into the world like a blank tablet; then through our experiences our minds start filling up, and we start learning things. But when we have dreams with images in them that we have never experienced before, we realize that there is something missing in that theory. So, symbols can be fascinating. However, they can also be frustrating, because how are we ever going to figure out what all those symbols mean?

When we see a play or read a story, we are exposed to a lot of symbolism, but often we don't think about it as such. When we experience a dream, it has a direct impact that we relate to. A movie would not be as effective if we just sat back and said, "Oh, they're showing me a lot of symbols here. I wonder what these symbols mean?" These are the things we talk about afterwards. While the movie is going on, we are really responding to the story; and it is having its desired effect. We are being affected by the symbols.

How does this work? How can symbols affect us if we don't know what they mean? Symbols remind us of things through association—they resonate with vague suggestions and we are reminded of a lot at an unconscious level. Some symbols trigger subtle, instinctive responses. For example, a snake is a very ancient symbol. It brings up a thousand images in our imagination, it immediately stimulates all kinds of fantasies. You can't say "snake means sex" or "snake means energy" because even if that were true, it is only partially true. We don't know what snake really means, but we really know it means something to us, many things, in fact! There is something going on that makes it possible for us to be affected by symbols that we don't even have in our experience. We can be moved by symbols, and yet if we are asked what a certain symbol means, we might not be able to explain it. What we could say about that symbol is small compared to how much it moves us.

So, association is one good way to explain how we seem to understand symbols. Another way is that we unconsciously empathize with the symbol. We imagine being that symbol. We might imagine what it would be like to unexpectedly encounter a snake when we hear the phrase, "He's like a snake in the grass," and something is triggered within us. We need to remember what we bring to a symbol. The expert symbolist Carl Jung would say we bring all of humanity's experience on the planet with us when we encounter that symbol.

It is quite interesting how Jung discovered archetypes and the collective unconscious. He was at a mental hospital, and a patient who was looking out the window called Jung over. He said, "Look! The sun has a tail and it's wagging in the wind." Jung had been reading about an ancient myth involving the solar

wind, and how the tail that wagged from the sun created the wind. So that was fresh on his mind. When
the patient had his "hallucination," Jung was really
struck by it. He knew the patient's background and
was willing to bet that this patient had never heard that
story and had never in his personal experience come
across that symbol. Yet he was experiencing it there in
the sky. From that Jung deduced that we bring with us
much more than what we have experienced in this life-
time.

In working with our dreams we can intentionally
empathize with any symbol in the dream. We can pretend we are that thing and see how we experience
things from that perspective. One reason that I believe
in Jung's view of the collective unconscious is that very
often in empathizing with a symbol we come up with
things that fit from a universal point of view, even
though from personal experience we don't have that
kind of knowledge.

I dreamt once that I was in a sporting goods store
looking at a glider—one of those sailplanes that glides
around without an engine. The man in the store told
me that there was a special sale on that day. If I were
to buy that plane, then for the rest of the time that I
owned it I could get two lifts a week into the air from
Penn Central. I thought that was really a neat idea
because, when you buy glider airplanes, you're still not
up in the sky. You have to find someone to get you up
there. So it was attractive to think that twice a week I
would get free pulls from Penn Central. And I saw a
locomotive going down the track, getting up speed,
with the little plane following until it picked up enough
speed to lift into the air. I spent a long time trying to
figure out that image. I kept trying to think of all the

things that I did twice a week, about planes and what they meant, of the goal-directedness of the locomotive. I came up with a lot of interesting ideas. Finally I took some time to empathize with the image—not just a mental empathy, but a physical empathy. I went outside and pretended I was a glider. I stretched out my arms and soared. I felt what it was like to be a glider airplane: very quiet, very free, moving about. Then I played a locomotive: going very straight down the track. A part of me didn't like it because I couldn't go off the track, but another part felt there was a lot of energy that was channeled because of the track. I could make big explosions inside, but I didn't have to worry because the track directed that energy and took me in the right direction.

Then I tried to imagine myself as a glider being pulled along in the air by a locomotive. I tried to do both at the same time, which was the image given me in the dream. It was quite an experience. All of a sudden I went into something similar to an altered state of consciousness. I could experience very directly the feeling of being both a body and a spirit simultaneously. I was in the world of cause and effect (which is like a train going down the track—once it's set in motion, it goes right on), and at the same time I was spirit, totally free, totally without materiality. They were simultaneous realities. I was given the immediate experience of it through empathizing with a dream symbol. I would never have suspected, just thinking about it, that this symbol could have had such potential and provided me such an important type of experience. Empathizing is a very natural thing to do. It does not require much expertise. You do not have to be a psychologist to do it. If children can get so much out of stories without having the stories explained, there must be ways for us to get great value from our dreams without having to know a lot.

Another important aspect of working with dreams as a theater experience is looking at the characters in our dreams. Even as in our daily life, stories in the dream involve things that happen between people. People are very important to us, and we know that in our dreams they often represent parts of ourselves. But I am more concerned with the conversations we can have with these characters than about what they represent. Just because a dream is over does not mean the story has to end. We can have continuing conversations with our dream characters. We have all probably had a conversation with someone and then later imagined how it could have gone differently. We ask ourselves, "What would have happened if I'd said this or that instead of what I did say?" It is just as natural after a dream to have imaginary conversation with the people in the dream.

I once had a dream in which I encountered a strong man who looked really mean. I walked over to him, wondering if he would bother me. He raised up his head and he was in chains. Rather than feeling safe and walking on, I said, "You'd better not bother me." He broke a bottle and threatened me with it, and I pulled out a knife. I wondered why if he was chained, I would be afraid of him, pick on him and try to start a fight. So I started talking to him and said, "That's funny, you're in chains and here I am picking a fight with you." He said, "Yeah, I know. You've kept me chained up all this time." I asked, "I've kept you chained up?" And he said, "Yeah, you don't want me to do very much. You have got all your stuff to do and you don't want to have any time for play; so you've got me chained up." We went back and forth. In the course of that conversation, he got me to agree to unchain him. What was interesting was that I had been feeling kind of low for a few days, and I hadn't been doing very much. What he was pointing out to me was that I was getting too mental. All of the things I was doing during the day were so mental that I wasn't allowing myself to go out and have some physical activity. He wanted to have fun. He wanted to use his body. He said that he would rake my leaves if I let him. I thought that was a good deal because I thought raking leaves was boring. So there was a combination of conversation, then a little empathy and role playing, and I became the strong man. I went into the yard and let him rake leaves and it felt really good to me. He was very good at raking, full of energy, and I found that I wasn't depressed anymore. It lifted me.

There is no great psychological expertise guiding that process, though from a psychological point of view, it made good sense. It was just me having a natural conversation with a dream character. Talking to him and hearing his suggestion was very helpful. I ended up painting a picture of him, unchained, to remind me always that all work and no play makes for a pretty boring life. So, conversing with dream characters is something we can all do. Gestalt psychology and Psychosynthesis both stress dialoguing, but we can bring so much psychology to the process that we forget we have a natural way of carrying on pretend conversations.

I want to remind you again that we are not stuck with how our dream ends. This is especially important with the so-called nightmare or with a dream that leaves us really troubled because of the ending. We can go back to the dream, while we are driving to work or washing dishes or whatever, and experiment with different ways of ending it. We can talk to different characters, get their ideas in the dream about what they might try, and even bring different characters in if we want. We are allowed to expand the range of people in the dream. This kind of an approach first really came to life with the Senoi Indians. They taught their children how to cope with negative figures in their dreams and how to bring dreams to a different ending. People think they have to study the Senoi method, but we don't have to study any method if we just allow our natural imagination to work on our dreams. We can just sit down with a dream and start playing with it. If we empathize with all the characters and let them speak, have some dialogue with them, try to shape the story and flesh it out, we can end up expanding a dream into a more elaborate and meaningful story.

This approach to dreams is a way of taking psychology and turning it into art. Psychology—in the sense of understanding ourselves, gaining better self-awareness, improving ourselves—need not be a process of gritting our teeth, need not be scratching our heads and trying to somehow figure out ourselves and life, as if it were all a big puzzle. Through natural ways of working with dreams, it is possible to move into the realm of arts and crafts and play and games and accomplish the same thing. It is a place where art and psychology cross over. The Greeks had their temples for healing and their temples for shared artistic experience in the same location. To them, healing and the arts were very much related to one another. We don't have to separate the two. We might look at opera, for example, as taking Primal Scream and raising it to an art form. The singers take all that emotion, channel it and make it beautiful. Our dreams are doing that as well, taking our touchy feelings, our intense emotions, and making drama out of them, so that we can experience our feelings in an aesthetic and meaningful way.

Beneath the surface appearance, there can be a lot of nature's own sophisticated psychology in our playing with our dreams. In their dramas and in their pantheon of gods, who often appeared in the dramas, the Greeks seemed to be paying tribute to the fact that unconscious feelings are like gods because they can take over and sway our lives. Such factors are eternally human and larger than life. When we dialogue with the scary people in our dreams, when we draw pictures of the images and symbols in our dreams, and then stand before them and imagine new conversations and scenarios, it is like we are wrestling with the gods in our lives. We pay them tribute and seek their blessings. It is only natural to do so.

CHAPTER FOUR

Dream Pillow

Do you have a problem or a difficult decision to make? As the saying goes, "Sleep on it!" Why do we say that? The saying does suggest, certainly, that during the night a dream, remembered or not, may resolve the problem or clarify the decision making. But why sleep *on* it? There does seem to be a literal aspect to the suggestion, as evidenced in some traditional practices. For example, there is the tradition that suggests that if a maiden sleeps with a piece of someone's wedding cake under her pillow she will dream of her own future husband. Another example comes from an article in *Time* magazine (September 20, 1976, pp. 94–5), where it was noted that when the Dalai Lama performed the three-day ritual of the "Sermon of the Wheel of Time," he gave each of his disciples two reeds to sleep on, one for under the pillow and one for under the mattress. He requested that they remember their dreams so that he could interpret them as part of the ceremony.

As a suggestion to dream, "sleep on it!" is an in-

triguing idea. I've tested it with hundreds of people, with mixed results. When the *Sundance Community Dream Journal* was introduced, a subscription flyer was mailed out with the suggestion that the potential subscriber first sleep on the flyer to see what the person's dream would say about subscribing to this journal on dreams. Many interesting dreams were received with the subscriptions. Of course, not everyone actually put something under their pillow to obtain the dream, but many people did. Believing in the practice isn't necessarily the most important factor in making it work. Several subscribers indicated that they thought the suggestion to sleep on the subscription flyer to be a silly idea, but, trying it anyway, they found that, much to their surprise, it worked! Similarly, in my workbook on how to obtain helpful dreams of guidance, *Dream Realizations*, I include instructions on writing a "pillow letter" to your dreams asking for help on the specific problem of concern, and then putting that letter under the pillow to sleep on it. In the feedback reports from the hundreds of people who have tested this workbook, again there was an indication that many people followed the instruction, in spite of their doubts about it, and found that it produced a dream. It often does seem to work, but how or why it works remains unclear. It's possible that by sleeping on something, a person is somehow reminded during the night of the intention to dream. It may be that putting something under the pillow acts like an auto-suggestion to dream, much in the same way leaving a notepad by the bedside is an auto-suggestion, saying, "I will dream tonight and I want to be ready to capture my dream!" It may be, on the other hand, one of those many aspects of relating to dreams where logic needs to be suspended in favor of symbolic behavior. Sleeping on something with the intent to dream may trigger an unconscious symbolic association with dreaming. In this respect, I find it a useful exercise for people whose rationality often gets in the way of their opening up to dreams. If I can get them to humble that rationality for a night by doing something that seems irrational, such as sleeping on a pillow letter, they often bypass that rationality and come up with a dream. I really don't know the why's and wherefore's of the matter, but while grown-ups often balk at the idea, the fact that children usually immediately find the idea an exciting one suggests to me that there may be indeed some innate symbolic connection between sleeping on something and dreaming about it.

A few years ago, a friend gave me a "dream pillow." It was stuffed with the herb, mugwort. I was told that mugwort would produce interesting dreams. Some time later, I decided to give the pillow a try. When I woke up the next morning, the room was flooded. The dream pillow, which had fallen on the floor, was like a used tea bag. Although I didn't have a dream, the flooded room seemed like a provocative symbolic event in itself. To me it evoked an image of "a flood from the unconscious," suggesting that the use of an herbal dream pillow could be a technique more powerful than I had ever suspected. I decided that it deserved some further, but more cautious, research.

A few months later, I received some more mugwort to make a dream pillow for my birthday. I made a pillow-covering myself, and my wife embroidered a dreamy design on it. As my birthday drew near, I gave serious thought to how to initiate my dream pillow. I couldn't accept the possibility that an herb would make my dreams for me. Anyway, I didn't want to operate on that principle. Then I realized that my nose never sleeps, and so the fragrance of the herb might serve as a constant reminder to dream. On the eve of my dream quest, therefore, I meditated with the dream pillow and put my nose in the pillow frequently during the day to establish a connection between the fragrance of the herb and my desire for a special dream. When I went to bed, I lay with my face right in the pillow and, as I breathed in the scent of the mug-wort, I repeated my petition for a dream. I let the scent carry the meaning of my intention to dream and carry me off to sleep with it. I don't know if I was actually aware of the scent all night, but it hit my nose in the morning and brought with it the most wonderful dream.

Since that time, I keep my dream pillow hidden away in a special box, to prevent its scent from attract-ing other associations. I bring out the pillow only on those important occasions when I have a special reason for dreaming. I now find that the scent of the mugwort has for me very distinct associations, bringing with it memories of those special events in my dream life. The fragrance now serves as a very intimate reminder of the connection between me and my dreams.

I still don't know if there is something special about the herb, mugwort. Perhaps other herbs would work as well, or even incense, as long as contact with the fragrance was restricted to occasions for dreaming. Whether using an herb, a letter to your dreams, or some special object or charm, I think the ritual of "sleeping on it" is something worth trying.

CHAPTER FIVE

Dream Incubation

Dream incubation is the ritual of going to sleep in a sacred place in anticipation of receiving a divinely inspired dream. Incubation rituals have existed in most older cultures where they are primarily used for guidance and healing.

The classic example, as I've mentioned before, is that of the dream temples of the Greek god Asklepios. A person with an illness would go to sleep in the temple. Asklepios would appear in a visionary dream to perform a symbolic operation or simply diagnose the illness and prescribe treatment, which the designated temple attendant, called *therapeutes*, would subsequently administer. Many testimonies concerning the healings and prescriptions which occurred in the dreams of those who slept in the sanctuaries of Asklepios exist today. The origins of some modern therapeutic methods have been attributed to these incubations.

Closer to home is the practice of incubation among various tribes of native American Indians. Their use of dream incubation has not been limited to healing. In

Mouse Flower

fact, many of their most significant cultural treasures are attributed to dreams received through incubation rituals. For example, Indian dream quests have often been discussed in connection with the rite of passage into adulthood. Among the Ojibwa of the Great Lakes the young person would go out into the wilderness and prepare a ritual nest where he or she would remain, fasting, until the anticipated dream was received. Usually their dream would contain some representative of the spirit world who would appear and bless the young person by revealing the youth's particular gifts and abilities, and would give instructions in the use of supernatural aids which might be available to the person in the future. Having been blessed by the dream, the young adult also would incur the responsibility of applying the gifts in a prescribed manner for the benefit of the community, often on penalty of contracting an untreatable illness.

The question uppermost in my mind was whether or not dream incubation was only a thing of the past. Could such events happen today? Most people today would not believe in the possibility of being healed in a dream by a god and not many would consider inviting a visitation from a spirit. Our modern worldview is simply not compatible with such events. Another approach would be necessary if I were to attempt to reconstruct a ritual of dream incubation in a modern setting. I decided to give it a try. It was at a summer camp for young adults that I then proceeded to try an experiment, setting up an aesthetically pleasing, dome-shaped tent to serve as the dream sanctuary. It was to be the focus of my efforts to re-create a dream incubation ceremony.

My guiding rationale in reconstructing the dream

incubation rituals were actually externalizations of internal, psychological processes. In other words, the dream incubation rituals mirror a natural inner process of self-regulation, healing and transformation. By aligning oneself with the symbolic structure of the ritual the incubant is able to allow a certain inner condition to arise which cannot be produced directly.

There were two major elements common to many incubation rituals: 1) the dreamer went to sleep in a sacred place, and 2) expected a helpful dream from a revered, divine benefactor. I assumed that these two focal symbols were actually projections of the incubant's own human potentiality. These symbols are operative today, for example, in some of our feelings and expectations concerning our personal spaces and vacation retreats, as well as churches and shrines, and even concerning our doctors, psychotherapists, clergy, or gurus. The essence of my reconstruction is the bootstrap operation of enlisting these current symbols of sanctity and power to form in the modern dreamer approximately the same psychodynamic configuration which must have existed in the psyche of the original incubant as he fell asleep in the sanctuary. In other words, I used modern symbols and procedures to place today's incubant in approximately an equivalent frame of mind as that presumably existent in the dream incubants of the historical past.

The procedure I developed was composed of four segments:

1) Selecting the dreamer for incubation.
2) Preparing the incubant.
3) Developing the incubation ceremony.
4) Receiving the incubant's testimony.

Selecting the Dreamer

In the temple of Asklepios, a dream incubation could not be sought until the person had been guided to seek such an experience in a prior dream. The incubants in my work taught me the importance of such timing. I came to use almost as stringent a selection criterion, not only to maximize the chances for the incubation of a meaningful dream, but also to protect the incubant from any feelings of failure. To maintain this strong factor of self-selection, there purposely was no solicitation for volunteers for this experimental incubation ritual. However, since many people inquired about participation, it became necessary to provide them with a means of still further self-selection on the basis of genuine readiness. The use of prior dreams as the basis of this selection suggested itself after I discovered that the most distinguishing characteristics of those incubants who had no dream recall the morning after the incubation ceremony was that they all had been unable to recall before the ceremony a recent dream related to the consciously stated problem they were seeking guidance on. Therefore, in subsequent incubations I asked potential incubants to rely on their dreams to provide the final basis of self-selection, giving an explanation such as this:

> "It's important that there exists the same readiness in the unconscious to work on the problem you've presented, as well as a genuine feeling of comfortableness about working with me and this incubation ritual. Since incubation involves the cooperation of your dreams, at least, I've found that it's safest and wisest to allow them to take the initiative

at this point. Spend some time thinking about your purpose for incubation, and see if your dreams concur by portraying in some form the problem you state for yourself. Should you decide that you would like to participate in the incubation ritual, bring me the dreams you remember."

Allowing the person's dreams an opportunity to respond to the prospect of incubation served well as a final source of self-selection. Many people who otherwise might have inappropriately participated in the ritual simply had no subsequent dream recall. The others returned with dreams portraying conflicts suggestive of the consciously stated problem. With a bolstered desire to experience the meaning of the suffering or inspiration which now had been both consciously and unconsciously expressed, all these people subsequently incubated meaningful dreams.

Preparing the Incubant

After the dreamer had an invitational dream to participate in the incubation ritual, a date was picked for the ceremony, usually from one to three days in the future. In the interim we proceeded to discuss the details of preparation. The preparation was perhaps the most important aspect of the ritual. It involved the incubant's contemplating the purpose of the incubation, choosing the personal symbols of the sacred place and the revered benefactor. They would also develop pictures representing these symbols and the dream from which the decision to incubate had been based. Finally, usually 24 hours before the incubation ceremony, they would spend some time in symbolic purification.

Here's how I instructed the incubants in these matters.

I first stressed the primary importance of mulling over the purpose of the incubation until as clear an image as possible was formed of the essential quest. I encouraged the incubant to devote sufficient time to activate and bring to consciousness all the feelings associated with this theme. I was especially concerned that the incubant give serious consideration to the secondary gains of his current problem or opportunity for which he or she sought a dream. I would also encourage them to consider consciously the various sources of positive incentive to a resolution of the situation. My instructions typically went like this:

> "As you contemplate your purpose, it is crucial you examine all the ways in which you may be possibly benefiting from your current situation of conflict. Search hard for such paradoxical benefits, and honestly consider your readiness to let go of those that may be incompatible with your purpose. If you can humbly accept your susceptibility to these sources of resistance, but you find yourself still willing to let go of their benefits, then you may open yourself to other resources which may offer genuine possibilities for change."

Such is the general tenor of what I tried to communicate to the incubant about the problems of the secondary gains of the present difficulty. To help prepare for receiving a truly insightful guidance from a dream, I also encouraged the incubant to consider the sources of positive incentive for change:

> "Summon all the reasons you can about the desirability of fulfilling your purpose. Savor what you wish to accomplish. Consider how accomplishing

your purpose will place you in greater harmony with life and your highest ideals. How have others been missing out on you and your special gifts because of your problem, and how will they be better served as you fulfill your purpose? But be sure to evaluate realistically your readiness to make use of the fruits of your incubation, so that you won't be hoping to profit by new possibilities that you can't actually implement. Perhaps the humble acceptance of your limitations may again be helpful in opening yourself to other resources."

These were issues that the incubant was to think about later during the preparation period while alone. However, I would provide some hints how the person might apply these general suggestions to whatever problem they were bringing to the dream quest. For instance, to a person wanting to overcome a lack of self-confidence in creative self-expression, I would propose that the person not only review all the facts and intuitions which affirmed the value of the person's creative gifts, but also search for possible fears of letting go of perfectionistic standards, and consider the readiness to assume the discipline and labor that all creative work requires.

I would also review the symbolic scenario of the incubation ritual with the incubant. We'd discuss how this ritual might be approached as a reflection of an inner process of self-guidance and healing, and how the incubant might best enter into the spirit of the ritual. Here I guided my coaching according to the metaphors the incubant provided, and I explained about the selection of the personal symbols of the sacred place and the revered benefactor:

"Your symbol of the place of sanctity should evoke a sense of reverence along with the feelings of safety, comfort and nurturance that this place provides. Search for such a place where you might go to think over an important problem, a place in which you feel you might be able to achieve significant perspectives on your life, a place where you would feel centered and at peace. For example, if you could imagine coming to a realization of the meaning of your life, what would be the setting in which this blessing would most likely occur?

"Your symbol of the revered benefactor should inspire you by the feelings of confidence, enthusiasm and optimism which this esteemed person evokes. Survey the people you have most respected and admired, people you have actually known, or only dreamed or fantasized about, and look for the trusted person who could best provide you with what you need to accomplish your purpose. Considering your own particular problem, find a person who you feel would have the right powers of healing, or a special quality of wisdom. Perhaps it would be someone loving and understanding, with a depth of perception which would enable that person to see into your heart and help you see yourself."

I advised the incubant to devote ample time to the contemplation of the chosen symbols. I also requested that pictures be made of these symbols to provide an external focus of contemplation to help the incubant develop a feeling of resonance with the sources of the projected images. I also requested that a picture be made of the invitational dream, which concerned the topic of conflict for which the incubation was being sought.

Finally, we discussed the significance of symbolic acts of purification and how such aspects of ritual may provide meaningful expressions of sincerity and receptivity. If the incubant was inclined to fasting, I suggested that it be approached not with an attitude of deprivation, but rather as an affirmation that one thing could be willingly sacrificed in order to allow sustenance from another source. Rather than necessarily fasting from food, I suggested fasting from an emotional attitude or habit pattern that would have to be relinquished anyway if the purpose of the incubation were to be fulfilled. I stressed that an effective fast need not be a perfect one. We can often learn a great deal from the difficulties of maintaining a fast. Discovering just how ubiquitous and unyielding to sacrifice an emotional pattern is can be humbling, and can also create more receptivity to the grace of the incubation. I also prompted the incubant to give special thought to the details of the physical preparation for the ceremony, such as bathing, grooming and clothing. These were all personal matters left to the discretion of the incubant. I did request that the incubant arrange the environment of the dream tent in a way that was personally pleasing, to placing prepared pictures in the tent in order to transform the space into the incubant's own symbolic sanctuary.

Instructing the dreamer in the details of the preparation typically required about an hour. I would then have little contact with the incubant until the evening of the ceremony. The day of the ceremony the incubant set aside as a quiet day of introspection.

The Incubation Ceremony

In the early evening the incubant and I would meet in the dream tent, spending a few minutes in silence together before beginning. To begin, I would ask the incubant to explain his or her purpose. I would simply listen to the ensuing story, asking an occasional question to clear the way for the expression of more subtle levels of meaning. I would specifically ask about the sources of incentives and inhibitions to achieving the purpose of the incubation. We would discuss the incubant's preparation for dealing with these matters, as well as with the possibility that the incubant might not remember any dreams. I would often counsel about the danger of expecting any particular dream experience. This initial period of the ceremony (lasting about two to four hours) functioned as an opportunity for cathartic confession, prompting the activation prior to sleep of many of the ideas and feelings associated with the incubant's purpose for this dream quest.

I would then ask the incubant to tell me the dream that had been brought to the ceremony, while we looked at the picture that had been made of this dream. We did not attempt to interpret the dream, but rather to sense the meaning of it. We alternated between empathic role-playing dialogues and analytical discussions. I'd encourage the incubant to play the role of each character or element in the dream. I'd even interview each character to elicit the expression of its own feelings and ideas. Then when we discussed again the possible meanings of the dream, the incubant would usually state that he or she now had a much more deeply felt meaning of the dream than initially. The incubant would also express some insight about the relationship between the dream and the consciously expressed problem, often viewing the problem from a fresh perspective.

Next, the incubant would resume role-playing the characters in the dream, this time engaging in switchback dialogue between the conflicting elements, while I acted as mediator. This was continued until some constructive resolution was achieved. By entering the dream emphatically and attempting to establish harmony, the incubant would experience how his or her variously conflicting motives, notions, habits and values resisted yielding to compromise. The struggle to carry the dream forward into harmony served as an affirmation of the incubant's willingness to explore new patterns. A key assumption underlying this part of the ceremony is that the incubant's symptoms respond sympathetically to constructive efforts applied in the domain of the dream symbols.

Eventually, I'd ask the incubant to assume the role of the person chosen as the symbol of the revered benefactor, using the picture made of the benefactor as a point of focus, or even as a mask. I would interview this person, eliciting enthusiastic expressions of the benefactor's self-confidence in such areas as healing, power and wisdom. When I would ask the benefactor to speak about the incubant's predicament, the benefactor would often speak with remarkable compassion and authority, offering surprising insights and suggestions. I then prompted the incubant to comment on the benefactor's remarks, and a fruitful dialogue frequently ensued. The incubant would be encouraged by the discovery of such a helpful resource.

Finally, I'd ask the incubant to describe the setting chosen as the personal symbol of the sacred place, while we looked at its picture. The incubant would assume the role of the sacred place, giving expression to those feelings that this symbol evoked.

The ceremony at this point would have lasted from four to six hours. There had been a progression of emotional themes, from the frustration, sadness or longing of the confession, through the conflictual turmoil and its resolution in the dream enactment, and finally to the optimism and serenity evoked by the personal symbols. I'd then inform the incubant that our work was essentially done, and we would take a needed break while he or she prepared for bed.

We concluded the ceremony with a pre-sleep reverie. While the incubant lay in bed, I began coaching in relaxation, giving instructions in experiencing heaviness and warmth in the limbs, and experiencing the breath as transpiring of its own accord and without personal effort. I included symbolic meanings with the instructions, and provided a symbolic context for the reverie, to place this practice in meaningful relation to the incubation process. "Letting go, trusting in inspiration" was the essential theme. I assured the incubant that having worked hard on the present problem, he or she could now relax. They could release the problem to the unconscious, and that just as one could trust one's breath, so could one trust to be inspired. Here is a partial rendition, giving the general sense of the instructional incantation:

"Hold your arm up slightly from the ground...
experience the effort required to resist the pull of gravity... gradually yield to gravity, allowing your arm to sink slowly back to earth... experience the pleasure of letting go, of giving in to gravity, of letting the earth support you... you have done all you can to work on your problem, and you are now entitled to relax... you relax as you allow yourself to experience your arms and legs as heavy... experience the pleasure of the sensation of heaviness as you let go of your problem and let the earth

support you . . . as you focus on the experience of warmth in your arms and legs you feel at peace . . . focus gently, gently on your breathing, following it in and out . . . as you exhale, let the breath go, and release yourself from the control of your breathing . . . give in to expiration with a peaceful sigh of relief, and then allow your next breath to come to you on its own . . . trust in your breath, and as you inhale, think, 'it breathes me' . . . let go of your breath and trust in inspiration . . ."

I then suggested that the incubant imagine being in the chosen place of sanctity, with the revered benefactor. The structure of meanings in the relaxation procedure and this suggested symbolic motif of the incubation process are mutually supportive:

"Imagine that you are in your sacred place. Allow the special protective and comforting atmosphere of your place of healing to create within you a mood of serenity . . . your arms and legs are heavy and warm, you have let go of your problem, yielding yourself to the support of the earth, giving in to your expirations with peaceful sighs, as you are safe within your sacred place of healing . . . imagine that your revered benefactor is approaching . . . feel the special vibrations of your benefactor's presence, and experience the confidence and optimism that is inspired in you . . . letting go with a peaceful sigh, trusting in inspiration."

When contemplated within the framework of all the preceding preparation, this final combination of images is assumed to create the receptivity appropriate for incubating a helpful and meaningful dream. To help the incubant maintain this receptivity upon falling asleep, I would then end the ceremony with a sleep-inducing reverie accomplished by music. I encouraged the incubant now to relinquish control of even the stream of consciousness, and while not trying to produce any particular result, fall asleep prepared and willing for whatever might be given.

"You are in the presence of your revered benefactor, safe within your sacred place, and have relinquished all further attempts to deal with your problem yourself. Give yourself over to anything that you might now experience, and assume that whatever you do experience is part of the healing that is beginning to transpire as you fall asleep. As the music plays, report to me whatever you experience, whether it be bodily sensations, thoughts, feelings or images. Let go of control over what happens from this moment on. Let go, and trust in inspiration."

I then turned on a cassette recording presenting a series of selections of classical music designed to be played during a reverie to enhance the emotional component of the reverie experience. This particular program, "Positive Affect," edited by music therapist Helen Bonny, has a sequence of emotional themes quite consistent with the symbolic situation being imaginatively assumed by the incubant. As the music played, I would simply coach the incubant to relay any experiences ("tell me what is happening now"), and as the incubant provided intermittent reports, I would reply with simple affirmative or supportive remarks ("fine," "go on," and such).

This final pre-sleep reverie was not intended to be an induced dream or guided fantasy, nor was it an attempt to program a particular dream experience. Induced, programmed or guided dream experiences may be very workable approaches, but are contrary to the spirit of this dream incubation ritual. Dream incubation progresses from preparation through hard work to surrender. The reverie and suggestive imagery were not intended as starting points for a dream, but rather to create within the incubant a particular state of being upon falling asleep. This state included an attitude of surrender and trust in inspiration. In order to free the sleep period and the dream activity to deal with deeper levels of significance, these techniques were used to discharge the surface material related to the incubant's work on this problem.

The music lasted for about 40 minutes, and by the time it finished, the incubant's reports would have become almost inaudible. I would then quietly leave the tent, while the incubant slept on.

The Testimony Session

The morning after the ceremony I would return to the dream tent and listen as the incubant related the dreams from the night. I would ask to hear the dreams at least twice, and then I'd ask about their possible meanings. In a manner similar to that employed the night before, I would coach the incubant in assuming the role of each dream element, and afterwards we would discuss again the possible meanings of the dreams and their relationship to the purpose of the incubation.

I cautioned the incubant not to be content with any particular interpretation or understanding, but tentatively to put into practice any supposed interpretation, allowing the meaning to develop over time. I also expressed my belief that the ultimate value of the dream might not in fact lie in its interpretation, but more in its direct experiential impact upon the dreamer—applying the dream in his or her life may reveal the meaning more than interpreting the dream. I would therefore suggest that the incubant mentally rehearse the dream frequently in the future to cultivate a resonance with its images. I specifically requested the incubant to make a picture of the dream to serve as a reminder and a focus of contemplation.

The incubant would then prepare a written testimony of the experience of the incubation ritual, beginning the account with our first contact. The testimony included a record of all the dreams recalled, from this first contact up until the time that the written testimony was completed. The testimony also included a description of the purpose of the incubation, the work that went into the preparation, and as detailed an account as possible of what occurred during the incubation ceremony.

Then I required the incubant to make a present for me. This was a symbolic gift that forgave the incubant of any obligation to me, appeasing any desire of mine for compensation and ending our ritual relationship as incubant and *therapeutes*.

Some Examples

In many incubations, the dream provided an intense emotional catharsis. For example, one man (29 years old) was frustrated by a work inhibition related to extreme self-criticism. This incubant had a prior dream which graphically portrayed the volcanic intensity of his creative energy, but which also portrayed his father as inhibiting the dreamer with his cynicism about his efforts to make use of this creativity. In his incubated dream, he had emotionally cathartic discussions with several important people from his past, including especially his father, from whom he received in the dream the kind of positive emotional support he claimed had been painfully absent in their relationship. The incubant awoke from the dream crying, but relieved and renewed, feeling a fresh capacity for creative work. At various times he would relive the emotional discussions that had occurred in his dream, finding them an ongoing source of encouragement and support for his work efforts. He also had some meaningful talks with his father. He felt these improved conversations were made possible because the dream experience released him from continuing his inappropriate emotional demands upon his father.

The incubated dreams often provided experiences that compensated for the influences of certain daytime experiences in the incubant's life. These compensatory experiences came in many forms. For example, one young boy (14 years), concerned with his involvement with psychedelic drugs, brought to the incubation ceremony an epic seafaring dream portraying the plight of some pitifully adrift, waterlogged creatures who longed desperately for dry land. The young incubant empathized with these creatures, and recognized in their desire for dry land his own longing for a sure-footed alternative to his psychedelic voyages. Yet he resented the pressures of socialization he encountered in the "straight" environment of home and school. His incubated dream gave him the needed experience of navigating satisfactorily on dry land: He was walking down a hot, dry road in the middle of a forest, the dust choking him, when he came to a dead end. He climbed up a tree to survey the surrounding forest, and spotted an axe a short distance away. He climbed down, picked up the axe, and began making his own trail through the forest. In contrast to the dry, dusty road, the path he cut for himself was cool and refreshing. Encouraged by this image of blazing his own trail, when he returned to school he successfully initiated his own study projects. His use of drugs declined significantly, and his subsequent dreams provided him with additional images of special implements, such as a jewel-studded sword, which he could add to the resources needed to pursue his individual path.

Sometimes the value of the incubated dream was in providing just such inspiring symbols. For example, one young woman (22 years) with asthma wished to improve her overly restricting relationship with her mother, a situation which she felt contributed to her asthmatic condition. The dream she brought to the ceremony portrayed a little girl held captive within a suffocating house belonging to an old woman who had recently died. When she enacted this dream, engaging in dialogue between the little girl and the house, she not only experienced the guilt feelings aroused by her inclination to leave her mother, but she also contacted her feelings of self-doubt about being independent, feelings echoed by her mother. In her incubated dream, an inspiring elderly lady presented her with a fantastically beautiful dress, and sent her away on an important mission. The incubant did sew dresses, and dresses were frequent dream images, but were usually either too sexy and revealing for her taste, or were shabby or overly modest. She said that the dress presented to her in her dream was perfect beyond her imagination. I encouraged her to paint a picture of this dress, and perhaps to sew a facsimile. Some time later I encountered her, working away from home, and she said she was taking less medication for her asthma. She showed me some beautiful paintings of her dream dress. She was hesitant actually to sew the dress just yet, but she described to me instances in which she would have previously been lacking in self-confidence, but that now she handled more easily, simply by imagining that she was wearing her dream dress and acting accordingly.

There have been incubations more ambiguous than the three examples given, as well as some more dramatic. In addition to their incubated dreams, certain incubants experienced something during the night which had the quality of a vision. In contrast to their incubated dreams, the content of these experiences did not seem to fit in with the themes being worked on, and were not the typical dreamlike dramas set in distant locales. Instead, the setting of the vision was within the tent itself, where the incubant was visited by a strange presence. The vision would end when the incubant awakened, but leaving the person confused whether the event really happened or was a dream. In one instance, an incubant experienced a beam of light emanating from the presence of someone standing outside the tent, and this light passed through the incubant's body, seemingly near his heart. In another instance, an incubant awoke hearing a voice say, "Roll over onto your right side and I will give you your number." When the incubant rolled over, the voice spoke the number. The incubant reported that he accepted the number, then fell back asleep, and had a dream in which he took his number to a special friend for interpretation. These visionlike experiences were quite reminiscent of the written accounts of the dream visions experienced by indigenous incubants of other cultures. A final incubation convinced me of the importance of these experiences, and led me to suspend conducting further incubations until I have had ample opportunity to evaluate the implications of such experiences for the pursuit of this research.

This particular incubation was conducted with an extremely intelligent and creative woman (26 years), and was distinguished by the responsiveness of her dreams to the prospect of incubation. During the period of preparation, she had dreams in which her personal symbols were portrayed for her, and in which she received guidance in other aspects of her preparation. The morning after the incubation ceremony she reported to me some meaningful dreams which have since seemed to fulfill the purpose of her incubation. But also she hesitatingly revealed that something else had happened that night as well: She awoke, startled to find that a strong wind was blowing, and that the tent had blown away. A small, old woman appeared, calling out the incubant's name, and commanded her to awaken and pay attention to what was about to happen. The woman said that she was preparing the incubant's body for death, and that the winds were spirits which would pass through her body to check the seven glands. The incubant was at first afraid, then took comfort in the old woman's aura of confidence and authority, and finally yielded her body to the experience, almost pleased with the prospect of death. During this time, the incubant saw before her a large luminous tablet, containing many columns of fine print, detailing her experiences in her past and future lives. The vision ended abruptly, and the incubant found herself lying within the tent, as if she had awakened from a dream. She reported that this experience was qualitatively different, however, from any of her other dreams or psychedelic experiences. In her most recent letter, written several months after her incubation, she said that her visionary experience effectively revealed to her how her existence is not dependent upon her physical body. She also reported that her dreams were just beginning to deal with the contents of this vision, after having finally terminated a long series of commentaries on the dreams she had incubated concerning her initial problem.

It is in this last respect that this particular incubation, as profound as it may prove to be, has been similar to the results of the others: Whatever potential benefits were provided by the incubated dream, they seemed to require patient cultivation before they began to manifest in actuality. The incubants have typically presented stories of gradual change, in which participation in the incubation ritual is given a timely and meaningful role, but certainly not an exclusive nor necessarily causal one. Most significantly, the incubants have frequently reported a subtle yet quite encouraging change in their relationship to their dreams. Their dreams appear more responsive, and there is a greater feeling of dialogue and cooperation, as subsequent dreams have guided the endeavor to apply the fruits of the incubated dream. The incubation ritual was designed to reflect back the incubant's own inner resources, and to help the incubant become more self-sufficient in growth. As one incubant phrased it, the incubation "gave me a unique touch with myself."

I'll conclude these observations by briefly noting that the dream tent also seemed to provide the community as a whole with a means of self-reflection and growth. One incubant had a dream about the community which, when enacted by its members, provided a meaningful symbolic psychodrama revealing existent patterns of interpersonal conflict and providing means of reconciliation, and which served to reintegrate creatively the individual incubant into the community. I also observed instances of apparently telepathic dreams, but particularly provocative were dreams of community members on the night of an incubation ceremony which went beyond telepathy to suggest that an individual incubant's healing dream involved a transformation for the entire community of dreamers.

CHAPTER SIX

Dreaming for Mary

Dreams are thought to be for the dreamer only. But that is not always the case. Sometimes dreams can be beneficial for other people besides the dreamer. In my first chapter, I described how a dream both helped me deal with alcoholism and also led to the development of a dream incubation procedure that was helpful for others, as you have seen. I would now like to describe for you another fascinating approach for getting help from dreams, involving *group* dream incubation. This procedure was also born of dreams, my own as well as others. Let me first describe the procedure as you might experience it for yourself.

Imagine, then, if you will, attending a "Dream Helper Ceremony." You are gathered with a group of people for an overnight healing service. The conductor of the ceremony explains that the group is going to dedicate their dreams that night to two people who are in need.

"Tonight, you will not be dreaming for yourself," announces the conductor, "but for someone else. You

The Dream Helper Ceremony

will discover your telepathic healing ability by putting it to work serving the needs of someone in distress."

The conductor explains that the group will divide and form two circles of "dream helpers" and will offer their dreams to two people in distress.

"Who among you is feeling particularly troubled," asks the conductor, "or is dealing with a specific life crisis and would be willing to ask this group for its help? You will not be asked to disclose tonight the nature of your problem. In fact, we wish you to keep it a secret until after we give you our dreams tomorrow morning. But tonight, as you sleep, you must be willing to open yourself to the healing energy of this group. As you consider whether or not you would like to be the focus of this healing service, keep in mind, that our dreams will go beyond the surface level of your problem, so do not ask for our help unless you sincerely are willing to examine the root of your concern."

Among the twelve or so people present, three or four persons gesture or step forward to indicate their desire to be the focus of the group's healing energy. A cast of lots determines the two persons toward whom the group will direct their dreams. The conductor asks for a silent prayer as the lots are cast, "May those two people most in need and who can best be helped by the type of healing service offered this evening be the ones who are chosen."

Once the two "target" people are chosen, the conductor addresses the rest of the group, saying, "As you look at these two individuals, tune in to your heart and ask yourself which person you seem most drawn to help. Trust your intuition." Then the two target people are asked to gather their belongings and to leave the room momentarily, with this instruction, "Search through your belongings for about six personal items, such as a piece of jewelry, a key, etc., that you might loan to your dream helpers for them to sleep with tonight, to help them better tune in to your energy. There is no need to try to clue anyone about the nature of your problem by your choice of objects, for the more we helpers are in the dark, the more we have to rely on a psychic connection to help you."

While these target people are out of the room, the conductor asks the group to divide up into two groups according to which target person they would like to help. If the groups are unequal, the conductor asks for volunteers from the larger group to move over to the other group. Usually there are sufficient numbers of helpers who are equally drawn to both target persons so that getting equally staffed groups is no problem.

The target people are then invited to return to the room and meet their group of helpers. The groups are asked to maintain silence and to prepare for a period of meditation. After the meditation, the target person distributes the personal objects to the helpers in the group.

The conductor provides little explanation for how to go about obtaining a dream for the target person beyond some simple reminders. "Take the object your target person has given you and sleep on it. Remember, tonight your dreams are not your own. You are donating them to help your target person. You don't have the right, then, to lose any of your dreams, so be prepared with a pad by your bed. Since the dreams belong to the target person, you don't have the right to censor your dreams. Even trivial details may be important. Bits of your dreams that might be embarrassing must nevertheless be reported—the dreams belong to the target person and those embarrassing details may very well be an important key to helping the target person with his problem, whatever it is."

If you can imagine being in such a dream helper group, you can appreciate how it might feel preparing for bed on such an occasion. You don't know what the person's problem is, but you are certainly curious and are trying to feel it out. You want to be helpful, but you just can't believe it would be possible for you to have a psychic dream that would be worth anything. The sense of curiosity, doubt and the atmosphere of expectant tension is part of the experience.

As part of the evening's preparation, the conductor explains the history of how the "Dream Helper" ceremony came to be, which helps provide a framework for the healing service and gives the participants some sense of the possibility of being able to help out with their dreams. I will give you some of that history now.

The story of this ceremony goes back to the days when I was conducting research on dream incubation, using the "dream tent" at a summer camp. Although the dream incubation tent was originally designed and presented as an individual and private healing ritual, as it became a significant event in the life of the camping community, the people sleeping in the dream tent became a natural focus for other people's dreams. Sometimes these peripheral dreams would appear to be a reflection of the dreamer's identification with the incubant. Other dreams would contain material which was indeed informative or helpful, as if such a dream were a commentary on the incubant's problem. I could easily regard these peripheral dreams as natural extensions of the supportive group atmosphere, involving normal, although extraordinarily intuitive, processes of interpersonal perception. Yet there would be those occasional dreams that would seem definitely of a psychic nature. For example, a dream might portray in such explicit detail a facet of the incubant's situation, something apparently unrelated to the dreamer's own life, and concerning something that the incubant had shared with no one, that a telepathic or clairvoyant interpretation seemed unavoidable.

As pleased as I was to observe such happenings, I was uncertain about how to render these events serviceable to parapsychological research. It was then my good fortune one summer to have Dr. Robert Van de Castle join me at camp. Bob is Professor of Psychiatry at the Medical School of the University of Virginia and has a background not only in dream telepathy experiments, but also with Native American Indian ceremonies, which proved to be particularly helpful. Bob also had prior experience at this summer camp and had observed himself that the community atmosphere favored rich parapsychological interactions among the participants. Bob and I discussed how to translate these phenomena into a suitable parapsychological experiment. We referred back to our experience consulting as parapsychological research advisors for the Association for Research and Enlightenment, the membership organization formed around the work of the late psychic, Edgar Cayce. During that consultation work, I had a dream that now seemed quite relevant to the task at hand.

The dream occurred after a day-long meeting of a committee of research advisors in Virginia Beach. The committee had been discussing how to meet the ideal of making research as enlightening for the participants as it was for the researchers. That is, we wanted to break away from traditional science, where "researchers" experiment on "subjects" who are usually kept in the dark about the purpose of the research and who thus play a relatively passive role in the pursuit of knowledge. We recognized that the "observer" and the "observed" affect one another and we wanted to design an approach to research that put both the researchers and the subjects into a cooperative venture of discovery. That night, I dreamed, "We are gathered together for research and enlightenment. We are standing in the dark, not knowing how to proceed. Suddenly, we begin dancing together, each of us displaying an individual symbol. As we greet and celebrate one another in turn, we realize our method, as the dance generates a fountain of sparks to light our path." At the time of this dream, we regarded it as an apt image of the research ideal we were seeking, but then gave the dream little more thought.

Later that same dream was to take on a second level of significance when it was made evident that it also portrayed an interesting experiment in group dream incubation, in which people pool their dreams to obtain guidance on a common problem. This process is similar to the American Indian ceremony, the Sun Dance. This dream led to the creation of Atlantic University's experimental publication, *The Sundance Community Dream Journal.* As the founding dream of that journal, it suggested how people might cooperate at the dream level to research topics of common interest.

As Bob and I reflected on that dream, we realized that it also spoke to the situation we were now confronting. If campers would spontaneously dream about someone sleeping in the dream tent, it seemed as if the camp community was naturally taking on that person as their common problem, making that person a focus of dreaming. My dream of the "research dance," therefore, seemed to suggest that these spontaneous happenings of clairvoyant dreaming might be brought under the umbrella of an intentional community event. And thus we designed the experimental "Dream Helper Ceremony."

So that is the dream history behind the ceremony. After telling this story, Bob usually shares the personal history behind his involvement in dream telepathy research. His stories are great fun, yet he speaks with authority. In Montague Ullman's book, *Dream Telepathy*, an entire chapter is devoted to Bob's telepathic abilities, where he is called the "Prince of the Percipients." Although Bob is primarily known for his work developing the "content analysis" method of dream interpretation and for his anthropological studies of parapsychology, he is actually the most thoroughly documented psychic dreamer on record. He can tell many amusing anecdotes to illustrate the important message that those frequently embarrassing details in a dream, seemingly initially irrelevant, often turn out to contain the biggest payoff.

Explaining this dream history and personal background in telepathic dream research brings some credibility to the bizarre experiment we propose to the group and serves to inspire them that perhaps it is indeed possible to have helpful dreams for other people. So, if you can imagine being in such a ceremony, you may suspect that as you go to bed that night, it is with some doubt, but some curiosity and anticipation as well.

The next morning the dreamers gather together after breakfast. There has been a sense of anticipation in the air, waiting for the groups to convene, to see what is in the dreams. When the groups meet, Bob and I have each led the group we dreamed with, and we survey people first to see how many people think they have had dreams related to the task at hand. Typically, very few people do. Most believe that their dreams could not possibly relate to the target person. Not until the dreams are told do the people begin to suspect that something is going on.

By way of example, let me describe some of the results of one dream helper group I conducted, dreaming for a 21-year-old woman, whom I'll call Mary. There were nine of us serving as helpers, but three persons recalled no dreams. One helper dreamed of going to a supermarket. Another dreamed of going to a drugstore to purchase a "pocket shower kit," but encountered difficulty paying for it. This helper also dreamed of going to a library. Another dreamed of a "Jewish Mother" who never believed her child was well. Another helper dreamed of holding hands in communion with Mary, of going to a piano recital, and of a boy diving very deep into a pool of clear water. Another dreamed of being under water, emerging to fly over our retreat, where she saw Mary and heard a doctor's voice declare, "Her diet is too tight—water is very important." This helper also dreamed of being at a fashionable poolside party.

I will report my own dreams in more detail. First, I dreamed that I was lying on the deck of a sinking ship. The water level was rising slowly, but was beginning to enter my mouth. I began to choke, and woke up abruptly, with the inexplicable impression that Mary had been ill and almost died. Second, I dreamed I was in my childhood home, and I heard "Mom" playing on the piano. I also saw her in the bathroom taking a shower. Then I saw her standing in the kitchen, dripping from the shower, talking on the telephone to someone about how her piano playing was always interrupted. I also saw "Dad" lounging in the living room in his pajamas. (I use quotes around "mom" and "dad" because they didn't look like my parents at all.) Then I went outside to return a book to the library. Outside on the lawn was my personal library, and it was being soaked by a lawn sprinkler. Those were the dreams for Mary.

As is usually the case, once all the dreams are reported, the group notices that they contain some common elements. It is the presence of common elements in the dream that encourages the helpers to accept the possibility that their individual dreams may be related to the target person. Before hearing from the target person, the group is encouraged to use these common themes to form some hypothesis about the target person's problem and its possible resolution.

In Mary's group, for example, certain images had been repeated: shopping, the library, mother, and piano. But especially was the image of water repeated, often in conjunction with a health theme. Putting our dreams together to form a pattern that might suggest the nature of Mary's problem, we speculated that Mary's problem concerned health, for which water might be a critical factor.

Now that the group has taken a stand and proposed to the target person their idea about the nature of the problem, the target person is allowed, for the first time, to open up and begin to respond to the dreams as they might relate to the problem or concern.

In our example, Mary was obviously stirred, and responded excitedly, saying something to the effect that we were wrong about the problem, but otherwise more right than we knew. She explained that the problem that she had sought help for concerned her recently canceled wedding. None of our dreams reflected a marriage theme, but two did touch on matters which were involved in the breakup. Mary recognized the dream of the poolside party as the type of social function she frequently had to attend with her ex-fiance and his family. She and he came from disparate social backgrounds, and this difference created problems for them. She said that the dream of the Jewish mother also reminded her of her ex-fiance, for he had once been very ill, and his mother continued to treat him like a sick little boy. Beyond these two correspondences, she saw little in the dreams pertaining to her question about the canceled wedding. Mary said that what so impressed her was to find so much in the dreams that was nevertheless directly related to many other problems that confronted her.

To the water imagery and health theme in the dreams, Mary responded strongly with an account of her medical history, a story she had not previously shared with anyone because of embarrassment. Mary had a chronic, epileptic-like condition, with seizure-like episodes brought on by tension. She said the themes of being under water reminded her of how she would feel "flooded" prior to a seizure, an image she had been concerned with during her stay at this A.R.E. retreat. She said that my drowning dream was a good image of what had happened to her during a recent stay in the hospital. As an unexpected side effect to some medication she had received for her condition, she developed a temporary partial paralysis in her sleep. As a result, while sleeping on her back, her saliva was not swallowed, but instead filled her throat, choking her, and she almost died from suffocation. My dream of going down with the ship seemed to me to be just the sort of nightmare of helplessness that might be provoked by an event in sleep such as Mary's. The resemblance startled me, because there was an unusual quality to my dream, and considering my impression upon awakening, I couldn't help but feel that I had somehow experienced Mary's hospital trauma. Be that as it may, I couldn't see how my dream could be of any help to Mary.

There was perhaps more help to be found in that other underwater dream, in which the dreamer emerged to fly over the retreat, see Mary, and hear a doctor comment on Mary's condition. Mary explained that her doctors had not yet diagnosed her condition to their satisfaction, and various treatment programs had been explored. The phrase, "diet too tight" reminded Mary of a related component of her medical condition —fluid retention—and she wondered if perhaps diet might indeed be a potential mode of therapy. Since Mary was anxious to reduce medication, perhaps this dream contained a needed clue for her treatment.

There were other areas of correspondence. Mary said that the image of a library had recently been on her mind. It related to her ambivalence about going back to school, because her parents would have to bear the expense. She frequently wondered why she couldn't learn what she really needed by reading in a library. It was interesting that my personal library, the one being watered in my dream, was actually borne out of just the sort of fantasy Mary had been entertaining. Concerning the piano theme, Mary said that everyone in her family was musical except her. She frequently went to piano recitals with her family. Her mother played the piano, but found the responsibilities of the home disruptive of her practice.

Mary's reactions to the dreams is typical of a target person's first response. No obvious "answer" is perceived, but many correspondences to related critical areas in the target person's life are recognized. This first level of response suggests that the group of dream helpers scored a number of "hits," or apparently accurate psychic perceptions. Are these correspondences more than coincidental? A typical experiment in parapsychology would stop at this point to focus on a statistical answer to this question, for it would be the crux of the experiment. The number of "hits" in this collection of dreams would be compared to the number of "hits" Mary might perceive in a collection of dreams that were actually unrelated to the experiment. In fact, Mark Thurston, Ph.D., Director of Research at A.R.E., in his doctoral research on a revised version of a dream helper ceremony, performed just such a statistical comparison to demonstrate that the normal scientific standards of "significance" can be applied, if desired, to the results.

As Bob and I originally conceived the Dream Helper ceremony, however, we wanted to test Edgar Cayce's suggestion that parapsychological research would uncover more meaningful information about the nature of telepathy if, instead of concentrating on "hits" (which tends to increase people's ego-involvement in the experiment at the expense of a more ego-free consciousness of oneness), we were to focus instead on how both the target person and the dream helpers are being served by the dreams. Cayce consistently maintained that behind the apparent psychic phenomenon in a dream, there was always an immediate and important purpose being served.

But what purpose was being served by our dreams for Mary? The purpose of the ceremony was to be helpful, not merely to spot isolated facts in Mary's life. It was at this point that Bob and I drew upon our understanding of psychoanalysis. Perhaps no other professional group has investigated parapsychological dreaming more than psychoanalysts. Like Cayce, research psychoanalysts have suggested that if an apparent telepathic dream is interpreted from the dreamer's point of view, then the underlying meaning of the dream will point to even more meaningful psychic connections than was originally suspected by simply comparing the dream to the apparent telepathic target.

In our group with Mary, for example, when I began the process of sharing my personal feelings about my dream, a more helpful pattern in the dreams emerged. In going over with Mary my dream of being back in my childhood home, we discovered that although our home situations had some commonalities, the dream depicted her home more than mine. Both our mothers played the piano, and both complained about their playing being so often interrupted. The physical description I gave of the mother in the dream was unlike my own, but fit Mary's mother very well. In my home there was only one phone, in a vestibule; but in Mary's home there were several, of which her mother used only the one in the kitchen. Whereas I recall my mother using the telephone but rarely, Mary said her mother was frequently in the kitchen talking on the telephone. Similarly, the description I gave of the father in the dream was unlike my own, but fit Mary's father well. The resemblance included his habit of lounging in the living room in his pajamas, something I don't recall my own father ever doing. This dream thus had the curious quality of being a literal representation of an aspect of Mary's home, but also portraying an emotional situation we both could recognize. If the literal details of the dream applied to Mary, I wondered if the emotional significance that might be revealed in the meaning of the dream might also be relevant to her. I therefore began to work on the dream relative to myself, to see if Mary would respond to any of my self-analysis.

The most salient aspect of the dream for me was seeing mother in the shower. This dream image recalled to mind an old childhood memory of walking in on my mother while she was taking a bath. I recall her getting terribly upset, complaining about her lack of privacy, and making me feel very guilty about invading her life. This memory seemed to have a strong emotional connection with memories surrounding my mother's piano playing. Listening to her play gave me an oceanic feeling of bliss. If she were to be interrupted, and get very upset, I would somehow feel guilty, as if I were the source of her frustrations, similar to when I interrupted her bath. From years I had spent in psychotherapy, I could recognize how such memories had been incorporated into my particular mother complex. One aspect was an unresolved dependency which was both disguised and fed by guilt feelings about being the cause of mother's unhappiness. It has been with the task of "watering my books," developing healthy reliable feeling ability to rejuvenate outmoded thinking patterns, that I have been forced to resolve this dependency.

Mary responded very strongly to my self-analysis. She explained that her mother's frustrations were a frequent source of friction in the home. Mary realized that she too, like me, assumed that she was somehow to blame for her mother's unhappiness and for the discord between her parents. Mary also now realized how her guilt feelings paradoxically inhibited any tendency to leave home and begin a life of her own, thereby prolonging her dependency. Mary indicated that recognizing her guilt feelings, her emotional dependency, and their relationship to one another, was a new realization for her.

Three other dream helpers supported this analysis by finding similar guilt and dependency themes reflected in their dreams. For example, the helper who dreamed of having difficulty paying for the pocket shower kit at the drugstore discovered that the theme of "paying for what you get" was exactly how she had to deal with her own difficulty in outgrowing her dependency on her mother. Mary responded to her by indicating that the library theme, which this helper had also dreamed about, represented the same type of problem for Mary, as she had not been able to face up to the responsibility of paying for her own education.

What emerged from the discussion was a definite pattern, reflected in the collection of dreams, revealing a hypothesis that Mary found very meaningful. Besides the possibility that diet might be a contributory factor in her medical situation, there was also a suggestion that there might be a psychosomatic component as well. Her feeling of being flooded, prior to seizure, echoed her style of dealing with emotional tensions, especially conflicts associated with guilt. Fantasies of guilt concerning her mother perhaps served to help Mary avoid assuming the responsibility for resolving her need for dependence upon her mother. Mary's ex-fiance appeared to have a similar dependency conflict, a commonality with Mary which seemed to have played a strong role in the breaking-off of their engagement.

The case of dreaming for Mary provides a good example of what happens in one of our experimental Dream Helper ceremonies. The group discussion becomes something like a self-help group session. The emotional sharing reveals how the dreams are both relevant to the target person's critical situation and to unresolved aspects of the dreamers' own lives as well.

The Dream Helper ceremony has been conducted on several occasions by Bob Van de Castle and myself, as well as by others, with similar results. It has served as the focus of research for at least two doctoral dissertations. It would appear that we have discovered that fabled unicorn, the "repeatable" telepathy experiment. But do the results of our dream experiment actually demonstrate telepathy? Whether or not our Dream Helper ceremony represents pure and simple telepathy is still unknown and will probably remain a difficult question to decide.

Turning our attention, instead, to the meaning of the results, we might ask first, how can we tell if the dreams and their interpretations actually contain pertinent information for the target person, or if what is really going on is a matter of reading into the dreams things that we want to see? Is it possible that we are *creating* meaningful correspondences rather than *discovering* them? One might argue that in matters of

112

meaning, creating it is as valid and necessary as discovering it. Yet we feel more comfortable if the meaning we see comes also from a source outside our own predelictions.

We have found what we believe to be a satisfactory answer to this question. It is the occurrence of commonalities in the dreams of a particular group, as compared with another group, that suggests that the dreams are in fact being focused on something specific to the target person. For example, in the case of Mary's group, several of the dreams contained the image of water. Now water is a very common dream image. However, while I was involved in that group with Mary, Bob was involved with another group, dreaming for another woman approximately Mary's own age. In that group's dreams, the image of water did not appear even once. However, that group had several dreams containing the theme of black/white and of related polarities. As it turned out, that target woman was concerned about a biracial marriage she was contemplating. In both cases, then, marriage was on the mind of the target person, but in Mary's group, the dreams apparently bypassed the marriage issue and focused on health and water as it related to Mary's health and her relationship with her mother, factors indirectly related to the canceled wedding. There were no black/white or polarity themes in the dreams for Mary.

When two groups are run simultaneously, it is easy to see how the dreams are focused and specific to the concerns of the target person. What can account for these differences except for the fact that the dreamers are focusing on the individual needs of the target person?

Sometimes, this type of difference can be critical to the healing potential of the ceremony. In one instance of Dream Helper that Bob and I conducted for an out-of-state workshop, I was in a group dreaming for a woman who was concerned about her repeated failures in career. The dreams for her contained repeated references to aggression, assaults and forbidden sex. It turned out that the target person had suspicions of being sexually molested as a child. One of the group's dreams correctly envisioned the circumstances of this event, in the cellar of the home. As it turned out, the central theme of the group's discussion had to do with how self-doubt and feelings of shame (in the target woman's case, related to the incidence of sexual abuse) contribute to blocks in creativity, an issue with which several people in our group were actively struggling.

In Bob's group, by way of contrast, the target person's question concerned the fate of her dead son. He had died under unusual circumstances and suspicions had been cast upon a person within the family unit. Although no evidence was ever obtained, and the death was ruled accidental, the cloud of doubt had persisted over the two years since the event. None of the dreams for this woman contained any images whatsoever of aggression, assault or foul play. Instead, there were several dreams involving tripping and accidents, and many references to natural disasters. The majority of the dreams also contained references to sons (but none to daughters), and there were references to crying and grief, questionable evidence, fires to put out and poor communications. What this group suggested was that the ruling of accidental death needed to be accepted so that the family could renew open communications and go on with its life. When our two groups met together to compare notes, Bob's

114

target person was impressed that whereas in our group there were many instances of aggression and foul play, in the dreams devoted to her question concerning foul play, not a single dream reflected that theme, but accidents and natural disasters instead. That comparison helped her accept the truth of the dreams for her that she should let the incident rest.

Another way of telling if the dreams are correct, or if we were simply confabulating the correspondences would be in the long-range impact of the ceremony upon the target person. In Mary's case, for example, she wrote back a year later. She had found an apartment for herself, was on a special diet and off medication. She had lost several pounds and was in a therapy group with her mother to work on their relationship. She indicated that the suggestions in the Dream Helper group proved very "on-target" and her application proved the interpretation, as Cayce suggested was the best test. In the case of the woman with the dead child, she wrote a letter to Bob indicating how she had felt such a load off her mind after the ceremony's conclusion. When she returned home, for the first time since the death two years ago, she discussed the matter with the family and they were now on the road to recovery from this tragic accident. This type of feedback seems to support the validity of the type of help that comes from the ceremony.

As a group activity, Dream Helper has much to recommend it. Besides giving people a taste of telepathy, it improves dream recall. We have noted that even with people who recall few dreams during a retreat, on the night of Dream Helper, recall is very high. It also tends to build group spirit and a sense of cooperation. This factor was tested experimentally by Alex Randall, who completed his doctoral research under the late

Margaret Mead by coming to one of our month-long workshops and collecting all dreams for the month. His study indicated that dream recall was highest that month on the night of the Dream Helper ceremony and that there were more group themes in the dreams that night than on any other night of the session.

The Dream Helper ceremony also raises a number of questions about the nature of dreaming, such as the extent to which dreaming is strictly a personal activity and the degree to which we may "meet" in our dreams. It also reveals how much commonality we share as human beings struggling with life issues. I suspect, in fact, that the Dream Helper ceremony will someday find its natural place as a family practice. Personal problems are often rooted within the family system itself, where the "identified patient" is often the focus of each family member's own projected problems. A family-oriented Dream Helper ceremony might well reveal the underlying "story" that binds the family to its "problem."

As I learned while dreaming for Mary, although my dreams invariably tell a story about me, they may also be pointing to something outside of myself. Yet following that dream pathway beyond my personal boundaries requires that I first have a good knowledge of what lies within me. Perhaps that is why Socrates advised to first, "know thyself!" As in my dream of the "research dance," where each person is offering something personal to the common goal, I have found it important to develop ways for people to know themselves through their dreams before they follow their dreams into the outer world. In the next section I share with you some of the methods I have developed for that purpose.

CHAPTER SEVEN

Dream Realization: Inspirational Writing in Your Dream Journal

My most satisfying moments of rapport with a dream have occurred when I stopped trying to interpret the dream, when I quit looking *at* it and began looking *with* it, trying to see the world in the way my dream sees it. While looking through a dream out into my life, as through a metaphorical looking-glass, I'll have flashes of lucid vision. "Aha! Of course!" I'm surprised by a recognition of the truths operative in my life, and I feel elevated into a superconscious awareness of meaning. The dream remains uninterpreted, but it doesn't matter. The dream becomes, not exactly understandable, but rather a poetic best expression of truth. The dream itself is transparent; it is life that glows with meaning. I'll be awed by the dream's uncanny ability to envision with images so personally suited to transform my experience. I then become

The Dreamer is a Dancing Tree

acutely aware of the Presence, of the "I am," and realize once again how, for "that that I am," a dream is a most natural mode of seeing.

In these encounters my dream brings no judgments. I feel neither guilt nor shame, pride nor power. I simply feel how I am. Meaning is. It is only afterward that I may respond with a judgment, perhaps with an automatic decision to persevere or to change course.

One day, the phrase "dream realization" came to me. I liked the sound of it, as it reminded me of "self-realization." Something like self-realization is what happens to me during those moments when, seeing through a dream, I realize the truth of the dream's ultraconscious vision, and I come into an awareness of the presence of the Self.

Reflecting on the processes that invite moments of dream realization, I have found that it is mentally re-experiencing the dream over and over again that returns me to that frame of mind from which the dream's perception arose. Also helpful is empathizing with the images of the dream, giving them voices with which to speak and eyes with which to see. Along with its images, the dream also has a story, a meaning within its narrative, having the thrust of an allegory, requiring only an instant to grasp. Experiencing my life in terms of the images and story of my dream, I am often granted metaphysical perceptions and discover that the dream envisions even the most mundane aspects of my life in mythic dimensions. I realize that the Self that I am, the dreamer and creator of my life, moves in an expanded, timeless consciousness, in contact with Olympus. The dreams become for me seeds which have fallen from the sky; and by nurturing them I grow to new heights of awareness.

Since the process of dream realization is difficult for

me to describe, I have worked to develop a more concrete approach. The result has been a special workbook teaching inspirational writing as a method of
dream interpretation. Titled, *Dream Realizations: A
Dream Incubation Workbook,* it includes many "meditations" for writing in a dream journal.

Keeping a dream journal is a tangible method for
providing a reflective atmosphere for communing with
dreams. Moreover, while journal writing involves processes that are easier to grasp, it also allows for the
elements of inspiration and surprise that are essential
to dream realization.

Inspirational Writing

Self-expository writing—writing about yourself and
your life—when focused through the imagery of your
dreams, can be a powerful tool of discovery. It does
require some practice, however, to develop a mental
attitude that best allows the inspiration to come
through in the writing. That is, even though we are all
familiar with writing, we can be prone to "writer's
block." To avoid this problem, you are encouraged to
practice "inspirational writing," a term coined by
Edgar Cayce to describe a writing form of meditation.

The easiest way to understand inspirational writing
is by observing your breathing and how it operates and
interacts with your awareness of it. Most of the time
during the day, and all night, you breathe quite normally, without having to pay any attention to it. Your
breathing is automatic. Now for a moment, pay attention to your breathing.

If you are like most people, once you begin to pay

attention to your breathing, you have the sensation that your are controlling your breath, the timing of the inhalation and the exhalation. Try to relax yourself for a moment, then gently observe your breathing and see if you can observe it without controlling it.

If you relax, and are patient enough, you will gradually begin to be able to simply witness your breathing as it happens all by itself, the way it happens all the time on its own when you are not paying any attention to it. Such a practice, observing your breathing without interfering with it, is actually an ancient form of meditation. If you practice it, you will find that during the exhalation, you let go and become very relaxed, and during the inhalation, you witness the mystery of inspiration! That the word "inspiration" is used for our breathing may give you a clue about inspiration as it is used in creativity. The processes are related.

Now let's consider three forms of writing. The first is "conscious, intentional writing." Very often it is like when you first try to observe your breathing: you feel you are in control, that you have to think up what to write, and you are conscious of your choice of words or of your lack of words to express what is on your mind. This type of writing we are all familiar with, and it is the type of writing you will be tempted to perform in the meditation exercises. You will read instructions like, "make up a sentence that uses the word, 'X'" and you will sit back and try to think up such a sentence, then write it down. Sometimes that will work and sometimes you will get stuck. Conscious, intentional writing is not the best kind of writing for this experiment in "Dream Realizations."

Consider another form of writing, "automatic writing." Just as we can breathe quite well without paying any attention to our breathing, so it is possible to write without paying any attention to our writing. By distracting, blocking, or blanking the mind, people have learned that it is possible to let the "unconscious speak directly" through their writing. Sometimes this approach to writing has been called "stream of consciousness writing." By whatever name, you are not being asked to attempt that form of writing. You don't have to learn to go into a trance to get your inspirations for your journal. Your dreams are your natural, creative trance state. When writing in your journal, you are encouraged to be alert, relaxed and aware, and to experiment with inspirational writing.

Inspirational writing is like gently observing your breathing without interfering with it. In fact, it helps to focus on your breathing for a moment, remind yourself that you can be aware of your breathing without stopping the flow, before you begin each writing exercise. With inspirational writing, you are aware of the purpose of the writing, and you are aware of what you write as you write it, but you experience the writing as almost happening by itself.

To perform inspirational writing, you reverse the usual procedure. Normally, as in conscious, intentional writing, you first think up what you want to say, then you record your thoughts. In inspirational writing, you do the reverse: you begin by writing, with your purpose in mind, and you observe what you write. You are not recording your thoughts on paper, but rather you are noting in awareness what you write.

It helps if you approach the meditations in inspirational writing in the spirit of fun and not allow your seriousness of purpose to make you up-tight. Don't look at your journal as a monument in which you will engrave your words of wisdom for all to read from now to eternity. Rather, look at your journal as a playground of learning. Like a playground, it is a safe place to experiment, to play with words and ideas, to "mess around." You don't have to be neat! Relax and enjoy your adventure.

Dream Journal Meditations

I have tested dream journal meditations orally with live audiences and in written form with participants in the A.R.E. Dream Research Project. I have observed that writing inspirationally in a dream journal meditation, though not inevitably promoting experiences of dream realization, often does give dreamers a sense of rapport with their dreams. Being convinced that this approach can be effective, I am confident in presenting one of these meditations to you for your experimentation.

Presenting the meditation in printed form, however, does pose certain problems. A dream journal meditation, as a form of inspirational writing, is best approached in innocence, without planning ahead. When the instructions are printed, the reader may look over the entire meditation first, and can become tempted to speculate and anticipate what might result. A more serious problem is that for some people the printed instructions arouse something like "test anxiety," eliciting concern about doing the meditation "correctly." Be assured that the instructions are meant to serve only as a guide. In this regard, let me share with you a dream related to me by someone who was working with some journal meditation instructions I had printed:

> "I am in a college . . . a hospital . . . hurrying up-
> stairs to talk to a friend on the top floor about a test
> I must take. I am afraid. It is a test where I must
> read problems and then translate them into formu-
> lae and work them out. During the test, the teacher,
> named Bonanza, says, Be quiet a moment and let
> me figure this out."

The dreamer appreciates the dream journal as being a place of learning and healing, and wisely seeks inspi-ration from the "friend upstairs." But the dreamer re-gards the meditation itself as a test, and is anxious about performing it correctly. I have to accept with good humor the dreamer's perception of the medita-tion instructions as being like "problems" with "for-mulae," and you may appreciate this simile yourself after you have experienced the meditation. I like the teacher's name because it aptly expresses the fruitful-ness of inspirational writing. The teacher gives some good advice: Simply be quiet and let the intelligence flow.

Learn from this dream. Approach the meditation not as a test or challenge to your skill, but rather as a game. Pretend that the meditation is not serious, and be playful, experimental. But also approach it quietly, remaining open to inspiration. Most of all, allow your-self to be surprised.

The Dream Realizations Meditation

1. Select a dream. The meditation works best with your ordinary, everyday type of dream, but falls short with those very special, highly symbolic dreams. A good bet is your most recent dream.

2. It's helpful to rewrite the dream in the present tense, as if the dream were happening right now. As you write, re-experience the feeling of the dream. It's also helpful to be quick and brief. A long dream may be effectively condensed. If details seem important write them out, but there is no need here to include details simply for their own sake.
Example Dream: "I walk past my friend's house and see a cat up in a tree. I look the cat in the eye and it winks at me. I wink back and walk on."

3. Read over the dream, and as you do, notice which words grab your attention. What words elicit a special response, touch on a sensitive nerve, or seem important? Underline about four to eight of these key words.
Example: Friend...Cat...Tree...Wink...Eye... Sly

4. Take each word in turn and allow it to develop into a truthful statement about yourself. That is, for each word, compose and write sentences about *yourself* using that word. This will get you behind your dream, looking through it out into your life. To get started, it may be helpful to pause for a moment and tune in to your breathing, until you can trust in inspiration.

126

Let the key word freely spark phrases and sentences about yourself and how you are living and experiencing your life. Use your pencil to play with the word, to discover the play on words, to experiment. Let your pencil do the writing while you ignore rules of grammar and spelling and simply meditate upon the feeling of the word. Be permissive with pencil rather than pushing. Be patient with the task at hand rather than demanding. If a particular word doesn't seem to yield sentences about yourself, try playing with rhymes and word games, jot down a few things the word reminds you of, or go on to the other words on your list and come back to this word later. But try to persist until you have written several meaningful sentences about yourself for each of the words you have underlined. If other thoughts and sentences come to you in the process, write them down too.

Write truthful and meaningful sentences about yourself, not about the word. For example, using the word "flower," don't write, "flowers are pretty." Instead, try something like, "I wish my creativity would begin to flower." If the word were a person's name, like "Mary," don't write, "Mary is my friend." Instead, try something like, "When I'm with Mary, I feel very confident about my abilities." Use the word in a sentence to say something important about yourself.

Example: "Sly: sly sly sly cat, sly sly, eye sly shy, I can be shy as well as sly ... sly eye, with my sly eye upon the world from a distance I can pretend that I'm on top of things, I can forget that I'm shy. Rather sly than shy, when shy I can cast a sly eye.

"Cat: cat, fat cat, contented unto itself, the cat reminds me of sly, of being self-contained, aloof in the tree winking at me, making me wonder ... I'm shy the cat is sly . . . I can be sly like a cat and act in a very self-contained manner, even when, especially when, I'm really feeling shy. A cat on a hot tin roof, easy does it. I can tread lightly as a cat when I sense trouble or possible danger."

Friend: I'm a friend, you're a friend . . . I can be a friend . . . I would like more friends . . . As a friend, I can be hard to reach but when you're with me you'll like me.

Tree: Tree, me, see, up a tree . . . I can be up a tree in my thoughts, afraid, or not knowing how to come down. The tree of my life branches out in too few directions.

Wink: In a wink, in a blink. I never wink but I blink. I can wink at some of my faults, I can blink at my mistakes.

Eye: The eye of the beholder. I am the eye of my beholding, the mirror of my self-awareness is the eye of my I-ness. Look into my eye and you make me aware of my "I."

5. Read over what you have written and make some additional notes about the themes and concerns that seem to be coming through. What seems to be on your mind?
Example: Having friends, being lonely, being shy and self-conscious. Being aloof. Acting sly, above it all.

6. Reread your dream and compose several different titles for it. To title your dream, focus on the essence of its story. Think of a phrase that captures the central theme of the dream. Write down several different titles until you arrive at one that you really like.
Example: "Sly Cat in a Tree Look-Out" or "The Winking Cat."

7. Take each dream title from your list of titles composed in the previous step and pretend that the dream title refers to you and your life. How could that title be about you? Write a statement that explains what the title might mean in relation to you.

Rather than thinking up something to write, then recording your thoughts, put your pen to paper and allow yourself to write whatever comes, observing your writing without controlling it. Allow your pen to be moved by your inner source of wisdom. While you focus on your dream title, let your moving pen do the thinking. Doodle with words.

Example: "Sly cat in a tree look-out": Sometimes I sneak off to gain perspective on things. Sometimes in a situation I will climb up my thoughts to achieve a good vantage point to view a situation with sly detachment, winking to myself that I do really understand what's going on around me.

"The Winking Cat": A wink suggests cleverness, a trick, a friendly conspiracy, a secret greeting. Sometimes when I am being sly or aloof, I can recognize my shyness that is behind it. Sometimes my cleverness, when I am using it to meet and greet people, will wink at me, at my shyness, as if to say, "We have them fooled, they don't see how shy you are because I am covering it up for you." Sometimes I am more aware of myself than I let on to myself.

8. As a final integrative act, take one of the titles you gave to your dream and use it as a theme for a brief essay or free-form poem about yourself. A good way to get started is to look through the material that you wrote during this meditation and note words and phrases that strike you as particularly meaningful or important. These could be either words or phrases

from your dream itself, words or phrases that you wrote about the key words in your dream, or what you wrote about the title or about what seemed to be on your mind. You can also use other words or phrases that occur to you as you play around with this material creating your poem.

Example: I can recognize my shyness—I am more aware of myself than I let on to myself—wink at me—climb up my thoughts to achieve a good vantage point to view a situation with sly detachment—a cat up in a tree—I can pretend that I'm on top of things, I can forget that I'm shy—contented unto itself—tread lightly as a cat when I sense trouble or possible danger—As a friend, I can be hard to reach but when you're with me you'll like me—up a tree in my thoughts, afraid, not knowing how to come down—I can wink at some of my faults—I am the eye of my beholding, the mirror of my self-awareness is the eye of my I-ness.

9. To write your poem, think of it as a brief arrangement of words that convey meaningful feelings, that capture or express some of the images that you've encountered in your work on Dream Realization. Don't be concerned about the format of the poem—rhyming and line length, etc.—but rather concentrate on finding words that match your feelings and imagery. Work with this material, changing it, adding to it and rearranging it; gradually mold it into a unified whole that expresses the theme of the dream title you have chosen. In other words, take the title of the dream and accept it as the title of an essay or poem that you will write about yourself. The raw materials for this essay or poem are contained in what you have written about yourself using the key words from your dream. All you

need to do is to edit your material, rearrange it, and form it into a coherent expression of the theme of your dream. The result will be a personal statement envisioning your life in terms of the images and story of your dream.

Example: "Sly Cat Up a Tree"

Sly cat up a tree—That is me.

When I sense trouble or possible danger

When I am shy

I climb up into my thoughts.

I can pretend I'm on top of things—

A good vantage point to view a situation with sly detachment.

Yet I am more aware of myself than I let on:

I wink to myself!

I am the eye of my beholding—

The mirror of my self-consciousness is the eye of my I-ness—

I can wink at my faults.

Up a tree in my thoughts—not knowing how to come down.

I can be hard to reach

But I think you'll like me if you can see me.

I can wink at you—

We may meet in a blink of an eye

Are we so different?

Our eyes may meet and wink at ourselves.

A conspiracy of silent friendship.

Slyness and shyness can be good friends.

Meditation Two: Opportunities for Dialogue

Symbols in a dream can be treated as projections of unconscious aspects of the dreamer's personality. We may then take advantage of the dream to gain consciousness of the symbolized attributes and how they function within us. The common method for doing so is the process of empathizing with the dream symbol, that is, experiencing the symbol from the symbol's point of view. Different traditions of dream interpretation have different methods of teaching this process. Gestalt therapy uses psychodramatic dialogue, where the dreamer enacts the role of the dream symbol, or alternates between two symbols, and engages in dialogue. In Psychosynthesis, the role-playing enactment is done through fantasy or reverie methods. Within the Jungian tradition, besides using fantasy, the use of artwork to express the symbol is also encouraged. Similar effects as those achieved by the above methods can also be achieved through inspirational writing in a dream journal, as has been demonstrated by Ira Progoff (see his book, *At a Journal Workshop: The Basic Text and Guide for Using the Intensive Journal*). What will be presented here are some specific ways for empathizing with dream symbols and engaging them in dialogue; this method is especially suitable for use in a dream journal.

To get the best advantage of a dream journal, recognize that it need not be merely a record of past facts and events, but can also be treated as a protected space, or playground, where psychological facts can be discovered and meaningful events can occur. The journal can be a living mirror for meeting yourself. For a journal to have such a living quality, it is helpful if you meditate briefly just before each spurt of writing. Ira Progoff suggests attuning yourself to the flow of spirit in your breathing, then allowing the same flow to transpire through your pen as you begin writing. A meditative approach puts you into a receptive frame of mind, preparing you to discover something new rather than merely to record old thoughts. When approached meditatively, writing in your dream journal can be a surprisingly inspired experience.

How to Begin

Getting started is often the hardest part. Here is a relatively easy way to get the process started. First, we have a dream. For example:

> I am swimming down a river. I see an inner tube floating across the river. There is a deer hiding in it. Reaching shore, the deer is confronted by a wolf. I swim to shore and catch them both in the inner tube, holding them close together. I sense a rising tension.

To get into the spirit of any particular dream symbol, simply rewrite the dream from the perspective of that symbol. This task gives you something specific to write about while "standing in the shoes" of the symbol and helps to get the empathic process flowing. To begin, read over your dream, pick a symbol, then close your eyes and try to re-visualize the dream as it would appear from the perspective of that symbol. With that orientation in mind, rewrite your dream. Begin with a statement, "I am . . ." and identify the symbol:

I am the deer. I am sneaking quietly across the river in an inner tube. When I reach the other side there is a wolf in front of me. Then a person comes out of the river and throws the inner tube over me and the wolf. Now I am face to face with the wolf— he is so near—and my heart beats fast with fear.

After the dream has been rewritten, you may continue the process by allowing the symbol to express itself: How does it feel about the events in the dream? What does it have to say to the other symbols in the dream? If you first meditate upon your breath, you may visualize your inhalations as bringing you the inspiration and awareness of the dream symbol and your exhalations as carrying this awareness to your pen as you begin writing.

I am a poor, frightened, innocent deer. I have few defenses except to hide. Crossing the water is very scary, for I am so vulnerable when I swim. Hiding in an inner tube, I felt safe crossing the water, but then, on the other side, I am confronted by a wolf. I'm sure he wants to harm me, to take advantage of me. I am about ready to run, but suddenly I am captured along with the wolf in the inner tube. What was once my hiding place is now my prison. Why have I been captured? What is going to happen now? You, person who captures me, why have you done this? Why don't you let me go?

Having the dream symbol express itself in such a manner usually paves the way for dialogue. But before we discuss approaches to dialogue, there are a few points to consider.

First, the process of empathizing with a dream symbol and allowing it to speak may sometimes be confused with automatic writing, a process that could lead to "dissociation" or "possession." Such confusion may create mental blocks for some people, inhibiting their ability or willingness to engage in empathic writing. But while automatic writing is a process that bypasses the conscious mind, the process of inspirational writing operates in cooperation with the conscious mind. When you write as if you were the symbol, you maintain awareness that you are giving permission to a part of you to express itself through the role of the symbol while you remain a silent witness. Inspirational writing operates in the direction of increased conscious awareness while at the same time allowing for spontaneous expression, making it quite similar to the process of meditation upon the natural flow of breathing. The intended effect is not entrancement but rather greater clarity of consciousness.

Second, since the purpose is to gain awareness of how the energy behind the symbol operates in your daily life, it is helpful at some point to reflect upon what has been written. See if what you learn from the symbol may be integrated into your conception of yourself. For example, with regard to what was written earlier by the "deer," I may reflect:

Deer . . . innocence . . . uses hiding as a defense . . . finds that his protection is now like a prison . . . how am I like a deer? . . . I am like the deer when . . . I pretend to be innocent . . . when I use innocence as a guise to protect me from criticism . . . when my defense of innocence prevents me from reaping the rewards of forthright risk-taking . . .

Generally, it is not a good idea to attempt to operate in both modes—empathic writing and reflection—

simultaneously. It is not advisable to analyze what you write while trying to let the empathic writing flow. But after a section of writing is completed, a period of reflective writing can be helpful to digest what has transpired and to guide the direction of the subsequent dialogues.

Finally, it is possible to work with each and every symbol in the dream, allowing each a chance to present the dream from its point of view and to express itself. How many symbols you choose to role play is up to you. Sometimes it is necessary to work with several symbols until one really begins to come alive with meaningful remarks that stimulate insight and lead to dialogue.

Dialogue

Dialoguing with dream symbols does not necessarily create an "interpretation" of the dream, but does provide an opportunity to interact with your inner life and to achieve a working alliance with it. It is not possible to prescribe exact methods and topics of dialogue that would be fruitful in all cases. But we can outline some general suggestions that may provide some idea of the possibilities.

We will discuss three approaches to dialogue. First, the dreamer dialogues with a symbol. Second, two or more symbols from the same dream dialogue with one another. Third, symbols from different dreams are found to set up special situations for dialogue. Each approach has its own particular usefulness.

Dialoguing ourselves with a dream symbol—the first approach—presents an opportunity for a more conscious and fruitful integration of the energy of that symbol into our lives. Sometimes we begin the dialogue with a discussion of the symbol's activity in the dream:

Deer: Why have you captured me here in this inner tube with the bad, mean wolf?

Me: I want to take a good look at you, deer. I captured the two of you to see what can be learned from this predicament.

Deer: But I'm innocent. Why won't you just let me go? It's the wolf that needs talking to—he's the bad guy.

Me: It was clever of you to use an inner tube to sneak across the river . . . clever as a fox . . . I can't believe that you are so innocent.

Deer: I needed to get across the river. I would have been very vulnerable swimming out in the open. The inner tube was a convenient coincidence.

Me: Why were you trying to swim over to the other side?

As the dialogue continues within the context of the dream situation, there may arise occasions for periods of reflective writing, when you attempt to formulate what is being learned. The dialogue may also leave the boundaries of the dream setting itself and begin to focus on how the symbol operates in your daily life. As you enter this domain, you may wish to negotiate a better working alliance with the symbol.

Deer: Now be careful with me, don't shock me with insight, as I am more useful to you as a quiet presence rather than as a blatant energy.

Me: Oh yeah? Tell me more about how you live within me. I see you as my characteristic defense of innocence, something that sometimes gets in the way of my taking bold steps.

Deer: Some things are better accomplished quietly; sometimes it is better for one hand not to know what the other hand is up to. I give you a quiet manner in the forest of life. The other creatures are not afraid to go about their business in my vicinity, and so, with my help, you learn more from others than you would if you presented a more aggressive face.

Me: I see what you mean, and I appreciate that quality. But sometimes, like you, I get too attached to my veneer of innocence, using it as a defense that actually inhibits me. Don't you ever come out of hiding, don't you ever assert yourself?

Deer: Yes, sometimes I can be a stag...

When dialoguing with a dream symbol, try to maintain a flexible attitude. For the purpose of growth or healing, it is sometimes necessary to be firm, sometimes yielding. If the symbol seems downtrodden, rejected, or repulsive, it is often necessary to be accepting and sympathetic, perhaps allowing the symbol to have a moment of catharsis—or even letting it tell you off!—before you can expect it to cooperate with you. Frightening or highly aggressive symbols require special strategies. All your skills in listening, negotiating, compromising and loving are relevant. Often you will discover that fairy tales, myths and biblical stories provide examples of how to deal with difficult situations. You may find yourself like a Daniel facing a lion, a David facing a Goliath, or a Princess kissing a toad. And like the Princess who kissed the toad, you may be rewarded by a surprise gift, such as an insightful statement about yourself or the discovery of a new talent.

One gift that is often helpful to ask for is that the symbol please come to your awareness during the day at times when it is active within you. For example, if the "deer" were to remind me of its presence every time I was using innocence as a defense in some situation, or when I needed to be more "invisible" in a situation, I could get a better feel for the activity of the deer in my life and learn to integrate it more creatively. Receiving such a gift could also lead to an ongoing relationship with that symbol and the special awareness it embodies. Remember, however, that symbols from the unconscious have the power of fascination, so be careful to retain an attitude of discernment when listening to what they say.

The second approach to dialogue involves having two or more symbols from the same dream speak with one another. Here is an opportunity to learn about the functional relationship between different psychological energies. There are usually many combinations within a dream, and which one you choose depends upon what you sense to be important or potentially fruitful. Conflict between symbols in a dream often means an opportunity for healing, to replace conflict with harmony, to reconcile an internal struggle between, for example, apparently opposed energies. In our dream example, the situation between the deer and the wolf provides an opportunity to resolve conflict. To get started, simply tune in to each symbol and let it express its viewpoint on the situation portrayed in the dream:

Deer: You wanton wolf, how horrible of you to lie in ambush for me, to want to do me harm.
Wolf: Delicious deer, it is simply my nature to

hunt for food and to snatch whatever tempts me.

Deer: We are so different. I am innocent, quiet and shy, while you are mean and aggressive.

Wolf: Perhaps, but if I eat you, then some of you will be in me.

Deer: It's hard to imagine your wanting some of my qualities.

Wolf: Everyone loves a deer, but who loves the wolf?

Deer: I'm not so popular when I sneak into a garden to eat the lettuce.

Wolf: But no one would shoot you for that, or leave traps around to catch you. It's our contrast that angers me, for you seem so innocent compared to me, and I seem too despicable compared to you. I'm really not such a bad sort.

The dialogue between symbols sometimes can go on and on without apparent effect. It may be useful to pause for a moment of reflective writing, to become aware of the significance of the dialogue. Afterwards, the dialogue may continue on another level:

In the dialogue between the deer and the wolf, I recognize a conflict I have between innocence and power. The wolf seems hurt because everyone hates him. This makes me think that part of my aversion to expressing power is that I don't want to be disliked by others. So I hide behind an image of innocence. But perhaps the wolf's power could bring out the stag in the deer. The deer's innocence might restore the wolf's aggression to a natural instinct for assertion and less one of revenge.

Me: Hey, you two, wolf and deer, perhaps you have something to offer one another and need not fight. Deer, can you find nothing to admire in the wolf?

Deer: I do like the way the wolf can walk in the

open without fear of attack. I admire his courage.

Wolf: I admire the kinship that the deer enjoys with the other animals in the forest. Sometimes a wolf's life is so lonely; I have only the moon to share my song.

Once conflicting symbols have expressed some willingness to exchange viewpoints, the process of reconciliation has begun. Continuing the dialogue, perhaps with intermissions of meditation and reflective writing, may lead to some compromise solutions. It is not necessary, however, to force the dialogue to a satisfactory conclusion. The process of reconciliation will continue silently within you, perhaps emerging in a new form in a later dream.

Sometimes a pair of conflicting symbols from a dream seem incapable of reconciliation, even when you step in yourself to try to help. Maybe you are too close to the conflict to offer the necessary diplomacy. If so, try the third approach to dialogue. Search among your other dreams for a symbol that might provide the necessary healing touch or at least a different attitude.

Laughing Woodsman: I am the laughing woodsman, at home in the woods and alive to the humor of its nature. Hey, what's this? A deer and a wolf caught in an inner tube? Ho ho ho! You two look mighty uncomfortable.

Deer: It's no joke!

Wolf: I didn't put us in this spot, believe me!

Woodsman: Ho ho ho! Here, wolf, let me pick you up and put you over my shoulder. You look mighty silly sitting there cuddling with the deer.

Wolf: I want to get back to my hunting.

Woodsman: We'll hunt together. We'd make a good team—once your anger wears off. You won't be lonely with me around. We can sing together. And you, deer, the next time you want to cross the river, allow yourself to float downstream as you slowly make your way across. That way, you'll blend with the current and you'll have the force of the river behind you.

Dialogue and Creative Writing

Experiment with different scenarios, using situations and symbols from various dreams, or create special situations, such as a courtroom, and let the symbols interact. Another special situation for dialogue is preparation for dream incubation (see Chapter Five). Take a dream symbol that represents an attribute in need of transformation to a symbolic place of healing. Empathize with that "place" and allow it to express its special vibrations. Introduce the supplicant symbol to your symbol of healing or wisdom and allow them to dialogue. Engaging in such inspirational writing before going to bed will often prepare you for the needed transformative dream.

Dream shields provide interesting starting points for expanded dialogues. My workbook, *Dream Realizations*, provides even more ways to use dialogues in a dream journal to explore beyond the horizons of the immediate dream material. What begins as an exercise in developing self-awareness transforms into an experience in creative writing. With patience and discernment, the dialogue with our symbolic life allows healing and art to become one in self-acceptance and expression.

CHAPTER EIGHT

Haiku Dream Realization

Gratitude to Edith Wallace

Somewhat like a moment of self-realization, when I can look through the eyes of my dream's ultraconscious vision and experience some truth—that for me is a dream realization. Creative writing, playing with the words in my dream record, often fosters dream realization. Sometimes it also provides an avenue of self-expression.

Dream realization and creativity require a relaxed, playful spirit. The limitations of a fixed form, however, may paradoxically stimulate such playful creativeness. As Rollo May suggests in his book, *The Courage to Create*, there can be no creativity without the presence of limits. If we are willing to accept and work with them, limitations breed transcendence. With that in mind, I offer a traditional form whose limits provide an excellent opportunity for dream realization through creative writing—the Haiku.

143

Haiku
Sev'nteen syllables
In lines of five, sev'n, five:
Image brings meaning.

I've found three applications for Haiku in dream work. First, in playing around with the words in my dream record, and with new words that come to mind as I try to fit my writing into the form constraints of Haiku, I discover new feelings about my dream images. In fact, Haiku is well suited to developing and expanding an impression of a single dream image or symbol into a full expression of meaning.

Ugly face monster:
Hate, anger, rage—tears of rage!
Your eyes crave my love

Second, Haiku may also be effectively used to condense an entire dream into a concentrated, seventeen-syllable vision. This type of condensation can be especially helpful in a dream group. Here we have many people who wish to share a dream and receive reactions from others. But time is limited. Also, in the usual telling of a dream, the dreamer often wanders through the story—sometimes backwards!—adding parenthetical remarks, explanations, and apologies along the way. If the dream is particularly long, the listeners can become confused. Certainly the emotional impact of the dream's vision is diluted, if not lost. I've found it to be a popular practice to take a few minutes at the beginning of a dream group session for each of us to prepare a Haiku version of our dream. We each then read our Haiku dream aloud and, after a moment of silence to let the dream touch us, reactions are generously forthcoming. We also find that the Haiku dream reveals the heart of the matter and thus quickly promotes fruitful discussion.

Finally, as a form of dream interpretation, Haiku dream realization can become an effective exercise in superimposing dream reality upon our ordinary vision. Here are the instructions I give: Condense the essence of the dream into the first two lines of the Haiku. Use the third line to convey some truth about your life that correlates with the dream's vision.

> *Mouse flower blooming,*
> *Unearth surprise, if you please.*
> *Shyness winks at me.*

Since this third Haiku exercise requires more patience and analysis, I encourage practice with the first two exercises, which can be more freely rendered. But if you can perceive in proper perspective the challenge of formal Haiku, a third line that presents an unexpected complement to the first two is both consistent with tradition and also yields valid dream realization.

CHAPTER NINE

The Dream Drawing
Story Game

We know more about the meaning of our dreams than we are aware of or can put into words. If we portray one of our dreams in a drawing, our hands will often reveal some of the meaning of the dream. At first, however, we are still too close to even our drawing of the dream to appreciate what our hands have revealed. It can be helpful to give our drawing to someone else and, not telling them the dream, ask them to make up a story about the drawing. The other person will unwittingly pick up on the clues our hands have left behind and these clues will influence the story that unfolds. The person's story may not particularly resemble the dream, but that doesn't matter. If we are attentive to our emotional reactions to the story as it is told, we might find that parts of the story, the words used, the themes and the descriptions of the characters will trigger flashes of recognition of the meanings in our dream.

THE DREAM TENT

That's the theory. Here's how it's done in practice:

The game begins by having each person in the group make a drawing of a dream. We allow perhaps 15 minutes for this, stressing that the purpose is not to create a work of art, but rather to express the theme, the action or the mood of the dream. The instructions are to make a single picture, not a series of cartoon frames. The picture may be representative of the dream to the last detail or simply an abstract expression of the dream. More important, however, is that people make drawings to suit themselves and not be concerned about how other people will react to them. Persons worried about their lack of "drawing ability" can be honestly reassured that it won't matter—they'll just have as much fun and get just as much out of it as the "artist."

While the dreams are being drawn, it is helpful if people are quiet, so that they can focus more energy into the drawings. It is also important that no one discuss or reveal the nature of the dream that is being drawn.

The finished drawings are collected and placed face down in the middle of the group. Then each person receives someone else's drawing without knowing, ideally, who the drawing belongs to. If the identity of the artist is known, we simply ask that this information be ignored.

Instructions are then given about making up a story about the drawing. It needs to be made clear that the object of the game is *not* to be able to guess what the dream was about. Instead, the purpose is to enter the drawing with imagination and emerge with a story that fits the drawing. Sometimes we say, "You can be most helpful to the dreamer if you simply let your imagination have free rein and if you can suspend critical judgment about your story-making skills." The instructions are that the story answer the following questions: (1) What is going on here? (2) What are the people, animals or things telling and thinking? (3) What led up to the present situation? (4) How does it all work out?

We give five minutes for people to meditate on the drawings. Then we begin to tell the stories. Each person in turn tells a story and, while other people may wish to comment or obtain further details of the story, the identity of the dreamer (the person who did the drawing) is not revealed. In this part of the game the focus is on the stories.

Sometimes the person telling the story needs some help. Helping the storyteller requires that the other people be sensitive to what is going on with the person as the story is told. Sometimes the storyteller lacks confidence, making only brief comments that don't quite form a story. The group can offer support, coaching by asking specific questions about the drawing until a story emerges. It is helpful to give reassurance that it is not the storytelling skill that helps the dreamer, but rather the person's willingness simply to tell what they are reminded of by the drawing. Should the story teller remark, "I don't know what is happening here; maybe these people are doing this, maybe they are doing that . . ." a helpful reminder is that it is not the purpose of the game to be able to guess what the dream was about, but to simply pretend that they *do* know what is going on in the *picture* and to tell the story.

Sometimes a person will not tell a story, but instead, will make evaluative comments about the dreamer who made the drawing: "The heaviness of these strokes shows that the dreamer is a very determined person." This kind of evaluation has to be curbed. Encourage the person to shift their sensitivity from the drawing style to the *story* they make up.

I make these comments only as a precaution, in case such problems arise, for they sometimes do. Yet for the most part, people have a natural tendency to make up a story about the drawing—it is child's play.

After the stories have been told, the dreamers identify themselves in turn, tell their dreams, and give their reactions to the stories. Sometimes the dreamer needs some help, too. It is natural to compare the original dream with the story told about the drawing. The dreamer may say, "Well, you were right about this part, but wrong about that part." That's fine, but misses the point of the game. The dreamer can be helped along with questions such as (1) What did you learn about your dream from hearing the person's story? (2) Did the story remind you or help you become aware of any feelings you had about your dream? (3) Did the story remind you of anything about yourself?

In the discussion period there are often discovered provocative connections between the story, the dream, the storyteller and the dreamer. It may be that the story's theme strikes a deep chord within the dreamer, perhaps revealing the essence of the meaning of the dream. More often it is just one aspect of the story that speaks to the dreamer, creating a new awareness about the meaning of some part of the dream. If the storyteller is asked to try to reconstruct how the drawing stimulated the story that was told, it may be learned that it was the color, the shading, the placement, etc. that seemed significant. The dreamer then may come to recognize the way he expressed himself with his hands and get in touch with new levels of meaning. Sometimes the story proves to be a remarkably accurate "reading" of the dreamer in some way, leaving the group marveling at the mystery of "where the story came from." There is no way of predicting in advance the kind of insights that will emerge from the discussion. So it is best to allow the discussion period to be freewheeling, led by curiosity and a respect for the truth contained in feelings.

At the end of the discussion period, it is important that people spend some time with themselves, writing in their journals about their experience. The purpose is to encourage people to "own" what they have learned. The story teller tells a story in "innocence." If the dreamer finds some truth in the story, it is truth recognized from within. Writing about what has been recognized will diminish any tendency to attribute the wisdom to someone else and make it easier to discard anything that doesn't really ring true.

Now I want to give two examples of my own dream drawings to show how the stories can be helpful.

The first drawing portrays a dream where I enter a restaurant and see a man seated alone at a table. Our eyes make contact and a woman's voice whispers in my ear that I should sit down at the table with the man. I refuse. The story that was told about this drawing concerned an artist at work in his studio. I forget the rest of the story, actually, because even at the time, it was the mention of "artist" that hit me strongly. Like most people, no doubt, I would like to develop the "artist" within me, so I was startled to suppose that the person in my dream whom I had rejected might have some-

154

thing to do with the artist. The storyteller explained that it was the "unkempt appearance" of the person in the drawing that had suggested the role of artist. That remark made me aware that in the dream it was the man's appearance that I had used as my excuse for not sitting with him. That moment of honesty led to further discoveries about how I cut off the flow of creativity by imposing arbitrary standards of social acceptability.

The second picture portrays a dream where I see a magazine ad for "Olympia" beer. I tear out the picture of the bottle of beer and eat it. The picture turns into a real bottle and I spit out pieces of glass. The story that was told concerned a person undergoing a period of purification. This person had gone to Mount Olympus to obtain special healing water. The water was having a purgative effect, inducing the person to vomit up the impurities in the body. In this story, it was the word "water" that rang the bell. The trademark slogan for Olympia beer is, "It's the water." I had "forgotten" that until the story was told, but then instantly realized that the slogan revealed the meaning of the dream. I had been in a process of trying to learn the meaning of alcohol in my life. In the dream I seem to be purging myself of any superficial or literal understanding, learning that by mistaking the image for the meaning, I would be incorporating something too concrete. I needed to purge myself of the "bottle" so that I could learn that it was really the "water" that I was seeking. Here is a good example of a story told in innocence that really hit the mark and had a healing effect.

Perhaps these two examples show something of the special value the dream drawing story game can have. What I like about it is that by telling a story about a drawing, most anyone can be helpful to the dreamer.

The game bypasses the intellect and relies on the intuitive processes in the storyteller. In this way, theoretical interpretations, which often result in making judgments about the dreamer, are avoided. Besides, any interpretation of a dream is really another dream about a dream. In the dream drawing story game this fact is "up front," for it is obvious that the story teller is making self-revelations in making up the story. Rather than by making diagnostic judgments, when people try to help one another by making self-revelations, the result is usually a more mutually supportive and healing atmosphere.

MEETING AT TABLE

"IT'S THE WATER."

CHAPTER TEN
Dream Shields

Dream symbols are like personal energy releasers. A group of symbols from several dreams can arrange themselves into a dynamic map of consciousness. Here we have the rudiments of a personal mythology.

The energizing effect of dream symbols is initially encountered in the context of the dream experience itself. Writing down the dream, reflecting upon it and enacting it are all means of cultivating the energy and consciousness-transforming power of the dream's symbols. Our eyes are especially sensitive to the vibrations of symbols and so it is helpful to render our dreams and their symbols into visual form. Drawing pictures of our dreams and keeping them within our view, such as posted by the bed or over the desk, transforms the dreams into personally suited *yantras*, visual meditations for working on consciousness.

But beyond drawing the dreams themselves, it is also valuable to collect symbols from various dreams and create collages, dream symbol mosaics. And by bringing together symbols from different dreams, a continuity in the dream-life is realized. We can begin to tell our story in the language of our dreams and discover the secrets of mythology.

There must be several different approaches to creating mosaics from dream symbols. For example, one may cut out pictures from magazines that are especially evocative of one's dream symbols. These pictures can then be arranged and rearranged, as in a game, to discover possible relations among the symbols. Or they can be chosen and placed at random, as if one had a personally suited Tarot deck for obtaining answers to questions. They can also be organized around a particular theme or arranged to tell a story.

Magazine cut-outs can be beautiful, but there are certain advantages to drawing our symbols ourselves. Our hands will express a certain knowledge of the symbol's meaning and with our eyes we can try to become aware of what our hands are telling us. We are also free to doodle with and around the symbols and join them in specially meaningful ways.

One approach to creating mosaics from dream symbols I call the dream shield. The shield is made in the shape of a circle. This imposes a certain structure, like a force field, so that making a dream shield feels like making a mandala. The shield is focused at the center and the natural symmetry suggests a situation of opposed but balanced elements. Like a mandala, the circular dream shield says, "These symbols are one."

A dream shield may be created to evoke a sense of identity, to express one's purpose in life, or simply to focus on a particular theme or question. The shield I've drawn here was created to help me understand one of my relationships with the Earth. Symbols related to this theme were taken from various dreams and released into the circle. They seemed to arrange themselves naturally. The finished shield provokes my imagination and prompts me to become conscious of its lesson.

Another value of a dream shield is that by collecting symbols from several different dreams, you can rise above the vision of the single dream and begin to see the story of your symbolic life as a whole. Also, the visual nature of the dream shield provides a potent focus for contemplation and further opportunity for you to be moved by the consciousness-transforming energies of your dream symbols.

Here I present an approach to making dream shields based on the theme and pattern of "the four directions."

What do you find within yourself at each of the four corners of the world? What is your understanding of the four sacred directions and how do you interpret them in terms of your own life? What symbols from your dreams would you choose to represent your feelings about the meaning of "north, south, east and west"?

Try making a dream shield that portrays your own symbolic orientation and relation to the "four directions." That is, pick symbols from your dreams that you think reflect these four archetypal quadrants of the psyche. Draw pictures of these symbols (or use magazine clippings) and arrange them into a circular mosaic that expresses your individual patterning of these four components of wholeness.

Suppose, for example, that you find the meaning of the four directions reflected in the four *elements*: earth, air, fire and water. You might try to make a dream shield that portrays your particular make-up of

Dream Shield: My Earth Symbols

Dream Shield: The Four Elements

Dream Shield: Amethyst Krystal

these four elements. Find symbols from your dreams that seem to symbolize the activities of these four elements in your life. Experimenting with different choices and combinations of dream symbols might reveal to you how, in some instances, the four elements of your nature work together harmoniously, while, in other instances, they are in conflict.

I've drawn up a playful dream shield on the theme of the four elements. Not knowing much about the deep meaning of the elemental symbols, I made a set of personal connotations: Air—minds, Water—emotion, Fire—spirit, and Earth—physical instincts. These personal associations enabled me to then find reminiscent symbols from my dreams: book, locomotive, sun and monkey. The shield that resulted teases me with its double message.

Here are two, wonderfully different, viewpoints of the quaternity, "the four directions." They may suggest additional approaches to constructing dream shields.

A beautiful rendering of a Native American worldview is given in the book, *Seven Arrows*, by Hyemeyohsts Storm. According to *Seven Arrows*, there are "four great powers" on the "medicine wheel" of life: *North* is the place of "wisdom," its color is white and it is represented by the Buffalo. *South* is the place of "innocence," its color is green and it is represented by the Mouse. *East* is the place of "illumination," its color is yellow and it is represented by the Eagle. *West* is the place of "introspection," its color is black and it is represented by the Bear.

These four "powers" confer "gifts" of perception. They are basic attitudes, or orientations, that people can use in perceiving and approaching life experiences. *Seven Arrows* teaches that each person is born in one of the four places and thus enters life with that particular power as his dominant gift of perception. It is then up to the person to "visit" the other three places so that the initial gift can be blended with the other three gifts of perception. Being a whole and complete person means having all four of the powers available to meet life and serve others. As an expression of wholeness, then, a dream shield can be a story map of your visit to the four places of "power."

Now although there is an archetypal pattern behind the association (as given in *Seven Arrows*) of the four "powers" with particular animals and colors, it is best for our purposes to consider these associations as just one of many possible choices. For example, in his *Dictionary of Symbols*, Cirlot reports that a traditional association in the Eastern world is as follows: *North*—black tortoise, *South*—red bird, *East*—blue dragon, and *West*—white tiger. For the Western world, Cirlot reports, there are the following animal associations: *North*—the ox, *South*—the eagle, *East*—the lion, and *West*—the peacock. I mention these differences to encourage you to come up with your own personal symbolic associations.

Our second example comes from the work of Carl Jung and his *Psychological Types*. Jung proposed a psychological analogy to the fourfold aspect of wholeness in his description of the four "functions." These four are thinking and feeling, intuition and sensation.

In this system, thinking and feeling are complementary, mutually exclusive modes of *evaluation*. When we evaluate by means of thinking function, we use external, objective criteria, such as logic. But when we evaluate by means of the feeling function, we use internal, subjective criteria, such as personal values and preferences. Often we are confronted with something that "makes sense" but that doesn't "feel right," or vice versa. Such apparent contradictions arise because thinking and feeling base their judgments on different sources of information, sources that are appropriate only to the particular function.

Intuition and sensation are the complementary, mutually exclusive modes of *obtaining information*. Their purpose is to discover what *is*, not to evaluate it. The intuitive function gathers information through subjective means of perception, such as hunches—it sniffs out the possible. The sensation function gathers information through objectively oriented modes of perception, such as the eyes and hands. For the sensation function, "beholding is believing," while the intuitive function believes in its dreams. A stone, to the sensation function, is a stone; while for the intuitive function, it might also be a paperweight, or even a companion.

Jung noted that everyone has all four functions operative in their lives. One function, however, is usually dominant from birth. Part of the life task is then to develop the abilities of the other three functions so that the four can operate as a harmonious whole. The function that is the most difficult to develop is the one that is complementary to the dominant function, for it is experienced as being opposed to that dominant function. For the person who approaches the world primarily through the feeling function, the thinking function is experienced as a cold and lifeless tyrant whose constant imposition of rationality feels like an irritating irrelevancy. The contrast is strong because the person has not yet visited the "place of wisdom" to learn of its positive "gift." And I purposefully use terminology from *Seven Arrows* here because it contains so many beautiful stories of the struggles and reconciliations of the four functions.

The person who is more comfortable with his thinking and sensation functions would find Jung's *Psychological Types* to be the illuminating exposition of the fourfold nature of wholeness. But those more comfortable with their feeling and intuitive functions would find the stories in *Seven Arrows* to be the more lucid revelation. I've tried to combine the two orientations in the dream shield I describe below.

At a dream workshop I once gave the following instructions for making a dream shield: Find symbols from your dreams that reflect the activities of the four functions—thinking, feeling, sensation and intuition—in your life. Arrange these symbols into a dream shield, with the symbol for your dominant function at the top of the shield and its complementary function at the bottom of the shield. Add whatever other dream symbols seem necessary to provide you with a sense of wholeness.

In the shield I drew (a later version is shown here) I began with the symbol of "sun" to reflect my intuitive function, the symbol of "tree" to reflect the most valued aspect of my sensation function, the symbol of "147" to reflect my thinking function, and "heart" to reflect my feeling function. By themselves on the shield, these four symbols seemed isolated from one another. So I began to add other dream symbols to reflect the ways in which the four functions operate together within me. The "dancing clown" touches the earth and also, through expressive movement, transforms his body into feeling. The dream symbol of the "star" reflects how, through geometry, my thinking and intuition functions become partners. And so it goes, around and around. At the psychological center of the shield is the symbol, "Amethyst Krystal." All together, the dance of the symbols on the shield forms a mask, a glimpse of a higher order of integration.

I share this shield with you as a way of suggesting how you might improvise on the basic, archetypal pattern of the fourfold One. It is worth the time to discover your individual symbols of the universal themes. Arranging your symbols into a dream mosaic also encourages you to begin to make up stories about how the symbols get along and adventure together. A dream shield can thus provide an initiation into your own mythic quest.

CHAPTER ELEVEN

Art of
Dream Realization

As a doorway, dreams present to each of us our own individualized invitation. For myself, one prospect that was inviting about dreams was their promise of providing seeds of creative impetus. I think of Thomas Edison, asleep in his laboratory. He gave the world a light bulb.

What is your light bulb to give to the world? It is said that each of us came into the world with a purpose, with something to give. The Native Americans honored this assumption with the tradition of the Vision Quest. "Go seek your dream," they would say to the adolescent, "and return to share with us who you are." The dream is a doorway to learn how to realize our intended innovations, our unique experiment in life, our gifts.

It has been on such an optimistic note that I have endeavored over the years to interest various people, community groups, businesses as well as schools in the

Meeting at Table

On the Way

creative potential of dreams. If creativity is an acceptable accent in which to engage people in dreams, then art is certainly a readily expected domain in which to experience that creativity. Although the same principles would apply to using dreams for sources of innovation in industry, for example, I have found it is easier to introduce the general concept by demonstrating innovations in art that have come from dreams.

One of the ways, in fact, that I myself have learned to realize what my dreams are showing me is through painting pictures. Besides prompting these pictures, my dreams also gave me some help in the actual techniques of painting with watercolors. While I present some of these paintings to you here, I will share with you some of my ideas about the use of dreams in art and in fostering creativity.

Dreams can be the inspiration for art. They can provide the impetus to create, the seed of what is to be created. For one thing, you can take a dream and draw it. Don't worry whether you think you can make your drawing look like how you remember seeing what was in your dream. Rather, think of someone you'd enjoy telling your dream to; only you can't tell it, you have to draw it. A dream is a story and a picture tells it. Dreaming, itself, is a process of drawing a picture, as in the slang expression for explaining the obvious, "Do I have to draw you a picture?" or as in the phrase, "drawing an analogy." So drawing a dream is an extension of dreaming, it is in support of dreaming. Drawing a dream is also one form of interpreting the dream.

The "Dream Drawing Story Game" I described earlier shows how to make use of the interpretive dimension of a dream drawing. Giving a person a drawing of your dream without telling him the dream but having him make up a story about the picture will give you a subjective, but definite, demonstration of just how much you have interpreted your dream in your drawing. My painting, "The Meeting," makes a good story about the potential impact of this process.

The original drawing of "The Meeting" appeared in the chapter about the "Story Game." The dream concerned my entering a restaurant and seeing a man sitting alone at a table. When given the drawing, someone told a story of an artist at work in his studio. Hearing the story, I was surprised to have the man labeled an artist—a placement on my scale of desirability just the opposite of how I had regarded the man in the dream. How could he be seen as an artist? What was I missing? Was it possible that by rejecting the scruffy and seemingly inept parts of myself I was turning away the opportunity to explore and develop my creative talents? My friend's story forced a re-evaluation of my dream, of that man and of my attitudes. For one thing, I decided to suspend my usual judgment of my doodles, designs and cartoons as awkward and inept, and allowed them to have more free rein in the expression of my feelings and intuitions. I treated this process with more respect and also invested in some art supplies. Without this dream, and its interpretation, I doubt if I ever would have become so dedicated in practicing artwork.

Drawing the story of a dream, turning a dream into a picture, is only one way to incorporate dreams into the subject matter of artwork. Simply the mood of a dream can instigate a painting. What two or three colors express the feeling in the dream? Would this color be big or small, pointy or rounded, concentrated or diffuse? How do the other colors fit in? Here we have the beginning of an abstract expression. Making an abstract expression is a good way to get in touch with one's moods and to discover the meaning of them. It doesn't have to be with marks on paper, however, as nonsense noises, for example, that express the mood can evolve into a song, or movements can evolve into a dance. The mood of a dream, or the feeling residual, can be the most lasting effect of a dream. Such a feeling can be difficult to put into words, and we are its captive until we can find some way to give expression to it that allows us to realize its meaning. We can use painting, singing, dance, even poetry, to get in touch with the feeling and, if we come up with a finished product that communicates a meaningful feeling to others, perhaps we have gone another step in the direction of art.

To supply the content for art, we don't have to use all the dream. A single dimension may suffice. It could be the mood. Sometimes a single image or symbol from a dream can be elaborated in a meaningful and powerful manner. That's what I've done in my painting, "Flowering." It is one image from one of my gardening dreams. In my chapter on "Haiku Dream Realization," I demonstrated the use of poetry for dream symbol elaboration by writing a Haiku poem about this flower, calling it a "Mouse Flower," to express its shy, but magical, qualities. There were no white dots in the dream, but in the painting, the white "twinklies" are a magical contrast to the flower's rather awkward lines of opening. I am still shy about my Mouse Flower; yet I did exhibit this painting and show it here to you.

Just as you don't have to use all of dream, so also do you not need to restrict yourself to a single dream, but may draw from many all at once. "Dream Shields," described in a previous chapter, are a simple way of combining dream symbols from many different dreams to create a visual statement. As explained in that chapter, a dream shield can be a mandala design using dream symbols as the content. A mandala is usually a statement about the self, but one can combine dream symbols—one's own symbolic vocabulary —to create statements about most anything. Linking dreams together in this way, with an implicit line or theme, is the beginning of thinking mythically—explaining or answering a question by telling a story composed of symbols from the unconscious. Perhaps such an approach produces an allegorical painting. Think of the juxtaposition of symbols in Magritte's paintings, or the boxed assemblages of Joseph Church.

I have also been concerned with the spiritual essence of art, having to do with the creative force, and helping people awaken to its presence in their lives. A spokesman for this point of view might be Frederick Franck, with his new book, *Art as a Way*: *A Return to the Spiritual Roots*. I also hearken back to the ancient Aztec tradition of the artist (toltecatl = "wise man and artist") as an ideal, much as we might use the phrase, "the Christ," to refer to an ideal, a potential, a pattern, a truth. In the Aztec tradition, to be an artist was to know God as sHe manifested uniquely in that artist's *heart* and to take all pains necessary to give truthful, and the most beautiful that the artist was capable of, testimony of that presence. The third year I was able to test this approach by working with three artists over an extended period to develop innovations and improvements in their artwork through the study of their dreams.

The use of dreams to develop innovations in the art technique excites me because it generalizes to innovations in other areas of life. What do we know, generally, about dreams and innovations? For the most part, from historical, anecdotal reports, they seem to come unbidden to a person who has been wrestling hard with a problem, and usually in very explicit form: in the dream, a solution or innovation is witnessed. I myself have had dreams that helped me innovate in my profession—experimental psychology of dreams—and in other areas, too, such as the watercolor paintings that are shown here—and some dreams of innovations came unbidden, others were incubated, some were explicit portrayals of the innovation, others required interpretation. What I have found about trying to share with others the possibilities for innovation through dreams is that the creative dreams of historical record —those unbidden and explicit dreams—do not inspire people, but leave them passive, waiting until the day they might be given such a dream. It also gives them an unrealistic goal, in that there is the impression that a creative dream is always distinguishable by its explicit portrayal of an innovation. Not that I would deny that the most cherished and valuable dreams may come unbidden and need no interpretation, but I do believe that it is important to start with what you have and work with it.

How I have worked with selected artists to help them innovate with their dreams is exactly how I have worked with anyone who was working on a problem and who was willing to allow dreams to make a statement about his work: What is your goal? What are the perceived obstacles to your reaching your goal? What solutions have you tried? In what ways have these solutions been satisfactory and in what ways have they been unsatisfactory? What will be the consequences of your achieving your goal? Are you afraid of any of the consequences? Are there any rules of procedure that you feel you must abide by in reaching your goal? What assumptions have you made about the nature of your problem that limit your choice of solutions? The answers to these sorts of questions help clarify the nature of the challenge the person has accepted and the meaning it has for the person. I assume that a work of art, like an invention, reflects the artist or the inventor, that the process of interaction between the artist and the raw materials reflects the artist as well as the materials, but that the creator is primary. When I take this perspective, then dreams become a natural helper, for dreams are meant to clear a path among the objective realities in life for the person's subjective, but true, self to come out and contribute to those objective realities. Again, it's that notion that everyone has a light bulb to contribute to the world, and dreams are waiting for us to ask for their help in finding and giving birth to that light bulb. So let's look at the dreams.

When working with someone on innovation and dreams, when we first look at the dreams, they seem to have little to do with the work issue at hand. To a large extent that is because most people separate their work issues from their personal issues, so all the feelings, worries, conflicts and other such typical dream contents, although they clearly relate, when interpreted, to the dreamer's personal life, don't seem to relate to their work issues, which seem to be issues of competence, pride, ignorance and acclaim. But when their personal issues are seen in a broader perspective, and when the answers to all the questions concerning the work goal are considered, it becomes clear that the personal issues and the work problems are both a part of the same core issues—discovering and risking being more of yourself.

I remember working with one artist, a ceramic designer, who was unsatisfied with the textures she was able to obtain on the bowls she was making. We spent a lot of time talking about what bowls meant to her; she had her private reasons, which she didn't feel were particularly relevant, as well as her public, professional rationale. One of her dreams involved a "shrimp boat." Discussion of that dream revealed a worry that she would "miss the boat," a concern she had about her life in general as well as about her art, a fear that she didn't have what it takes, or had the "wrong stuff," and would get left behind. I had the impression that she had the "right stuff," but was sitting on it because it didn't match what she thought was expected, what would gain recognition from her "art audience." She was approaching her work left-handed, as it were, since she kept her better hand behind her back. When we got to talking about shrimp, I noticed that although she said she didn't like them, she was able to describe their texture in some detail. It seemed as if she had some energy invested in the shrimp texture, so I suggested that she explore this texture in her ceramics. Out of this exploration came a new textural vocabulary which she developed in her work. As part of this artistic breakthrough came also more self-acceptance and confidence concerning the value of her own inclinations. The professional and personal dimensions grew simultaneously.

Confidence to be more yourself in your work—that seems to be the most general result of working with dreams to enhance creativity—which allows our naturally innovative nature to express itself. It was that way with my own work.

I had begun by drawing my dreams, using magic markers for color, doing so primarily to commemorate them and to allow me to reflect upon them directly. I didn't feel I could "draw," as these dream drawings didn't look anything like my dreams. But they "felt" right, and that seems to be what mattered at the time. Then someone gave me a set of watercolors. I tried them out, found them fun, but difficult to use. I did what I could with them, rather enjoyed using a brush and a box of colors, and was fascinated by what happened on the paper. Yet it seemed difficult to express any intention through the watercolors. But then I had a dream.

> I am in a movie theater looking at a large painting projected on the screen. The painting is like a large stained glass window, the surface area being divided into discrete areas, each filled with color. I hear my father's voice telling me that I can paint like that.

I used this dream as a basis for simplifying my approach to learning watercolors. By taking a piece of paper, drawing a design on it, then filling in the spaces with color, I learned how to apply color to paper in a smooth and even manner. I learned how to mix colors and how adjacent colors affected each other. I also learned how to build up color from several different coats of paint. Although this approach to watercolor painting is somewhat trite, it did enable me to learn some basic skills and gain confidence. It was as if my dream was saying, "Look, I know you feel over-whelmed by the complexity of watercolors, so why don't you try it this way for a while?" One of my favorite paintings, "On the Way," emerged several years later from this dream.

During the time that I was practicing this approach, I was also attempting to learn how to paint directly onto the paper. I was watching how my practice in the disciplined approach would affect my more spontaneous painting. I would fill my brush with color and begin making marks on paper. I would allow these marks to dry and then fill up with another color and make more marks, on top of the previous ones at times. I was concentrating on watching the various colors build up and interact and had learned how to paint on top of paint without getting "mud." I had another dream.

I am painting under the supervision of a dream teacher. I am making marks on paper in a rather spontaneous manner. When I am finished, my teacher asks me to examine the painting to see what I would see. I notice a figure implicit in the random marks, much the same way I might see something in an ink blot, and experience a strong emotional reaction to the discovery. My teacher says that when I encounter such an emotional reaction, I'll know I've found something.

This dream encouraged me to pursue painting in the manner I had been exploring. The importance of feeling was emphasized in the dream, as well as the process of discovery. The dream also marked another breakthrough for me. It suggested that although I didn't feel confident about setting out to paint "something," if I would simply put the brush to paper, make little marks, focus on the sensory effects of the color, then something would probably emerge from these marks that would give me a definite feeling of recognition. I used this method of painting for several years, primarily as a psychological tool. If I was in a mood and wanted to explore it, I would paint marks on paper until I felt finished, examine the result until some figure emerged that spoke to my mood. I also found that this approach was a good one for painting in the mood of a dream, and the resulting figures that I responded to would often help me understand the import of the dream. These paintings were quite personal—I called them my "psychological studies," and were not suitable for showing to others. Wanting to honor this dream, however, I painted "Dionysos" using this method. As intricate and planned as it looks, it began by some random marks and continued in this manner until a figure appeared, which I then built up in increasing detail using the overlay method I had developed.

When I was asked to be the subject of a Dream Art Exhibit, I was concerned that somehow exhibiting my work would jinx my continued enjoyment of painting. Perhaps I was simply nervous and self-conscious, not thinking of myself as an artist-for-show but instead more an artist in spirit. For most of the three months I spent preparing for the exhibit, I had no dreams. I would have been a very frustrating subject for one of my experiments. But as I was getting more and more of my old paintings framed, and having a chance to reflect upon how important it has been to me to have the opportunity to paint, my focus shifted to my message to others: "Just as I had lacked confidence in my ability and had been inspired by my dreams, so can you be inspired by your dreams." Then, a week before the show, I dreamed that the exhibit was opening, and that I was outside, painting an invitation to the show on the sidewalk. I awoke from this dream and immediately painted a sketch of how I was painting on the sidewalk. Then I was able to complete a finished painting in that style for the exhibit (not shown here). I was grateful that my dreams had provided me with something new to work on. Then, on the morning of the opening, I awoke with another painting in my mind. I painted that in my dream journal and realized that for me the process of dreaming and painting would continue as an ongoing exploration. This last dream removed my doubts and made it possible for me to be present at the opening of my exhibit, answer questions and share my delight at the work.

It is difficult for me to form an evaluation of these paintings in terms of artistic standards. From a psychological standpoint, I believe I see something of merit in them. I see something of myself in these paintings, something I like. Some of my friends who are professional artists say that they value the unique quality with which the watercolors are imbued, something they say reminds them of what is special about me to them. It sounds trite in words, and maybe all that is being reflected is love, or perhaps spirit. At another level, I can see how the paintings reflect something of my psychology. These paintings are not the flowing, expressionistic happenings that are often associated with watercolors at their finest. On the other hand, although there is a precision to the paintings, they did emerge somewhat spontaneously, like a doodle, and are full of expression. I see the paintings reflect an integration of a longstanding polarity within me, between planning and being spontaneous, evidencing an ability to arrive at a dimly perceived goal through a long process of successive approximations, which is a combination of both intentionality and chance. Such integrations I value, and have my dreams to thank for them in many areas of my life.

Getting help from my dreams has seemed to involve my being opened to innovative modes of perception as well as the feeling of greater self-acceptance. Dreams knit together the contradictory and conflicting aspects of my personality in ways that I could never have invented myself. As when my first dream slowly taught me the value of the rejected potato chips and mayonnaise, so later dreams have given me the confidence to let go of any limited notion of how I "should" be and discover instead how I actually am created—in the image of the Maker. Each of us is creative, each in a unique way. Dreams seem to want to help us discover that there is a whole lot more to us than we ever suspected.

Although they need to be approached and treated with the respect due a sovereignty, dreams are not really an end in themselves. Their secret is that they are but a doorway to a more valid and meaningful perception of life than we normally obtain through our scientific education. Dreams provide us with an innate, alternative education, and do so simply by working on our consciousness with stories that affect us at a deep emotional level. The greatest truths lie within us and come to the surface in our dreams. We needn't agonize over these dreams, trying to break their code. There is no code. They are simply stories we need to remember and to bring into our lives in a variety of natural ways.

In that way they can guide us, not only in our own search for happiness, but also in our efforts to prepare a better world in these difficult and threatening times. I can think of no other renewable resource that is as universally available for developing that vital link to nature's own invisible laws and purposes and to the spirit's activity within us than getting help from our dreams.

Dionysos

ABOUT THE AUTHOR

After receiving his doctorate from UCLA, Henry Reed developed research courses in Humanistic Psychology while serving as a psychology professor at Princeton University and designed dream research for the Carl Jung Dream Laboratory in Zurich. In recent years, he designed a modern Dream Incubation Method that led to many of his novel approaches to dreams. He also created and edited one of the most unusual journals ever published, SUNDANCE COMMUNITY DREAM JOURNAL, in which subscribers participated as a circle of dreamers. He is one of the most inventive dream researchers of our generation. With an innate appreciation of the visions of earlier cultures, he says he continues "to follow the path of the turtle and wait upon the bear."

For more information about Henry Reed's Personal Dream Quest Workbook, please write to him at the following address:

Henry Reed, Ph.D.
503 Lake Drive
Virginia Beach, VA 23451